LITERATURE FROM CRESCENT MOON PUBLISHING

Sexing Hardy: Thomas Hardy and Feminism
by Margaret Elvy

Thomas Hardy's Jude the Obscure: A Critical Study
by Margaret Elvy

Thomas Hardy's Tess of the d'Urbervilles: A Critical Study
by Margaret Elvy

Stepping Forward: Essays, Lectures and Interviews
by Wolfgang Iser

Andrea Dworkin
by Jeremy Mark Robinson

German Romantic Poetry: Goethe, Novalis, Heine, Holderlin
by Carol Appleby

D.H. Lawrence: Infinite Sensual Violence
by M.K. Pace

D.H. Lawrence: Symbolic Landscapes
by Jane Foster

Samuel Beckett Goes Into the Silence
by Jeremy Mark Robinson

In the Dim Void: Samuel Beckett's Late Trilogy: Company, Ill Seen, Ill Said and Worstward Ho
by Gregory Johns

Andre Gide: Fiction and Fervour in the Novels
by Jeremy Mark Robinson

Amorous Life: John Cowper Powys and the Manifestation of Affectivity
by H.W. Fawkner

Postmodern Powys: New Essays on John Cowper Powys
by Joe Boulter

Rethinking Powys: Critical Essays on John Cowper Powys
edited by Jeremy Mark Robinson

Thomas Hardy and John Cowper Powys: Wessex Revisited
by Jeremy Mark Robinson

Julia Kristeva: Art, Love, Melancholy, Philosophy, Semiotics
by Kelly Ives

Luce Irigaray: Lips, Kissing, and the Politics of Sexual Difference
by Kelly Ives

Helene Cixous I Love You: The Jouissance of Writing
by Kelly Ives

Emily Dickinson: *Selected Poems*
selected and introduced by Miriam Chalk

Petrarch, Dante and the Troubadours: The Religion of Love and Poetry
by Cassidy Hughes

Dante: *Selections From the Vita Nuova*
translated by Thomas Okey

Friedrich Holderlin: *Selected Poems*
translated by Michael Hamburger

Walking In Cornwall
by Ursula Le Guin

RILKE

Space, Essence and Angels In the Poetry of Rainer Maria Rilke

RILKE

Space, Essence and Angels In the Poetry of Rainer Maria Rilke

JEREMY MARK ROBINSON

CRESCENT MOON

First published 1993. Second edition 2020.
© Jeremy Mark Robinson

Design by Radiance Graphics
Set in Book Antiqua 10 on 14pt.

The right of Jeremy Robinson to be identified as the author of this book has been asserted generally in accordance with sections 77 and 78 of the Copyright, Designs and Patents Act 1988.

All rights reserved. No part of this book may be reprinted or reproduced, stored in a retrieval system, or transmitted, in any form or by any means, electronic, mechanical, photocopying, recording or otherwise, without permission from the publisher.

British Library Cataloguing in Publication data

Rilke, Rainer Maria, 1875-1926
Rilke
I. Title II. Robinson, Jeremy Mark
831.9'12

ISBN-13 9781861717818

Crescent Moon Publishing
P.O. Box 1312,
Maidstone, Kent
ME14 5XU, Great Britain
www.crmoon.com

CONTENTS

    Acknowledgements ✸ 9
    Abbreviations ✸ 11

1   Poetry ✸ 15
2   Space ✸ 41
3   Essence ✸ 58
4   Angels ✸ 70
5   Goddess ✸ 79
6   Symbols ✸ 94
7   Conclusion ✸ 101

    Illustrations ✸ 122
    Notes ✸ 128
    Bibliography ✸ 133

ACKNOWLEDGEMENTS

To Michael Hamburger; Peter Jay; Insel Verlag, Frankfurt am Main, Germany.

Footnotes are in square brackets: [1].

ABBREVIATIONS

SW	*Selected Works*
SaW	*Sämtliche Werke*, 4 vols
NP	*New Poems*
R	*The Rodin Book*
P	*A Ringing Glass: A Life of Rainer Maria Rilke*, by D. Prater
BH	*Poems From the Book of Hours*, tr. B. Deutsch
BI	*The Book of Images*, tr. E. Snow
DE/L	*Duino Elegies*, tr. J.B. Leishman
DE/C	*Duino Elegies*, tr. S. Cohn
SO/L	*Sonnets to Orpheus* tr. J.B. Leishman
SO/N	*Sonnets to Orpheus*, tr. L. Norris & A. Keele
LP	*Later Poems*, tr. J.B. Leishman
R	*Requiem and Other Poems*, tr. J.B. Leishman
P/26	*Poems, 1906-1926*, tr. J.B. Leishman
UR	*An Unofficial Rilke*, tr. M. Hamburger
Mit	*The Selected Poems of Rainer Maria Rilke*, tr. S. Mitchell
SP/L	*Selected Poems, tr.* J.B. Leishman
SP/B	*Selected Poems*, tr. R. Bly
RBR	*Rilke: Between Roots*, tr. R. Lesser
BR	*The Best of Rilke*, tr. W. Arndt
Lem	*Poems*, tr. J. Lemont
Mood	*On Love and Other Difficulties*, tr. J.J.L. Mood
Nor	*Translations from the Poetry of Rainer Maria Rilke*, tr. M.D. Herter Norton
Cez	*Letters on Cézanne*
LYP	*Letters to a Young Poet*
LM	*Letters to Merline, 1919-1922*
LTT	*Letters to Princess Marie von Thurn und Taxis*
LB	*Letters to Benvenuta*
Muz	*Briefe aus Muzot, 1921-1926*
Lou	*Briefwechsel Rainer Maria Rilke und Lou Andreas-Salomé*

RILKE

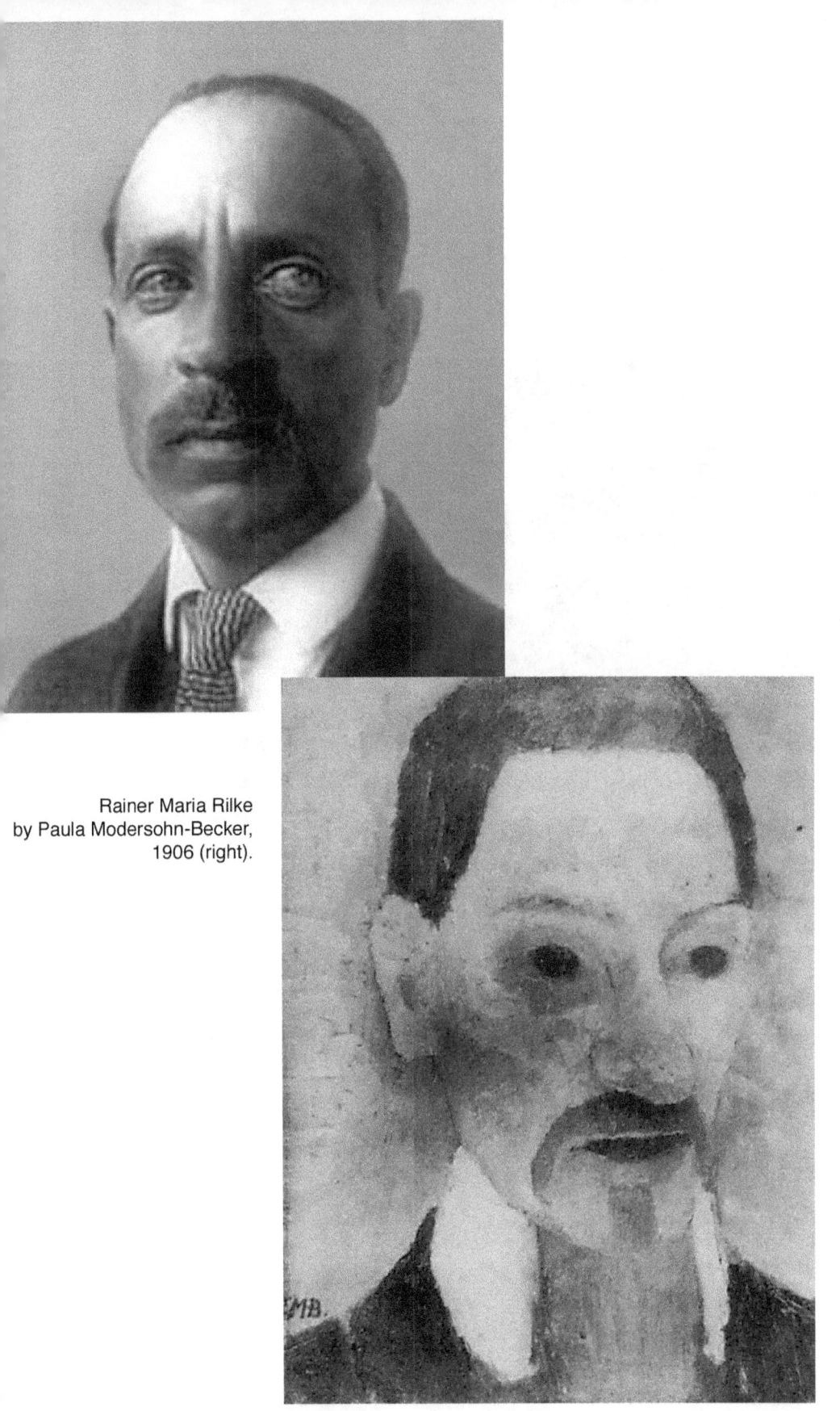

Rainer Maria Rilke
by Paula Modersohn-Becker,
1906 (right).

Rainer Maria Rilke and Clara Westhoff in 1904

ONE

POETRY

For verses are not, as people imagine, simply feelings (those one has really enough), – they are experiences.

Rainer Maria Rilke, *Malte Laurids Brigge* (26)

Works of art are always the result of having been at risk, of having pursued an experience to the very end, beyond which no one can go.

Rainer Maria Rilke, letter [1]

Rainer Maria Rilke (born René Karl Wilhelm Johann Josef Maria Rilke in Prague on December 4, 1875, and died in December 29, 1926 in Valmont) is one of the great, modern poets. He is beside Paul Valéry, Stefan George, Paul Claudel, Jules Laforgue, Guillaume Apollinaire, W.B. Yeats, Arthur Rimbaud, Stéphane Mallarmé and Georg Trakl. Rilke's world is that of Middle Europe, of Prague, Vienna, and German-speaking Czechoslovakia, of Franz Kafka, Robert Musil, Egon Schiele, Ludwig Wittgenstein, Karl Kraus, and Paul Celan. Rilke had an acute sense of homelessness, and he was ever restless. One of the main elements of his life is his rootlessness, his wandering across Europe. He is in his lifestyle one of the romantic, bourgeois, Europe outsiders, a figure familiar from the works of J.-K. Huysmans, Jean-Paul Sartre, Albert Camus, André Gide, Knut Hamsun, Fyodor Dostoievsky, D.H. Lawrence, Thomas Mann, Hermann Hesse, Thomas Hardy and E.M. Forster. Rilke's life fascinates readers and critics. It's easy to see why. There is the travelling, for example, around the cultural capitals of Europa; there is the *mittel* European heritage; the friendships with powerful personalities such as Lou Andreas-Salomé, Princess Marie von Thurn und Taxis, Auguste Rodin, André Gide and Paul Valéry; the etherealized romances and liaisons; the copious letters (which greatly assist biographers); the flux of his ideas; and his mysterious character, which is never quite fully revealed by any amount of biographical detective work.

Rainer Maria Rilke is one of those artists, like Leonardo da Vinci, William Shakespeare and Vincent van Gogh, about whom legends grow. Rilke is eulogized as a saint, a mystic, a martyr, a prophet of an age. Like certain writers (Ludwig Wittgenstein, Friedrich Nietzsche, Fyodor Dostoievsky), Rilke is thought to have something really profound to say about life. This is true – but his ambivalence and ontological ambiguity remained active to the end of his life. He never resolved the many conflicts in his life, just as Francesco Petrarch and William Shakespeare didn't: they too remained in a state of flux, dissatisfaction, imbalance.

Rainer Maria Rilke was very sensitive to all sorts of things – people, places, atmospheres. He picked up influences from all over. People, especially, influenced him – one thinks of Auguste Rodin, for instance. After the influence has reached its height, Rilke absorbs it, and forgets it.

There are many muses in Rainer Maria Rilke's life – women with whom he was passionately involved (tho' often thru letters).

RILKE

Rilke's deep relationships stem largely from a supra-sexual, idealized communication. Rilke's biography is a litany of muses: Merline, Marie von Thurn und Taxis, Magda, Sidie Nadherny, Clara, Lou Andreas-Salomé, 'Nike', and heroines such as the Virgin Mary, Mary Magdalene, Eurydice and Alcestis. Few major poets have had so many women friends, so many relationships with so many muses. Rilke is one of the most feminized of important modern poets, but at the same time he was deeply ambivalent in his attitudes towards women. He feared and desired them, wishing to come close yet also to remain at a safe, controllable distance.

Although Rainer Maria Rilke disliked being termed a German artist, he was clearly part of the German literary tradition, as embodied in the idealism of philosophers such as Immanuel Kant, in the pessimistic, *via negativa* mysticism and piquancy of Arthur Schopenhauer, in the tragic arrogance of Friedrich Nietzsche, in the dialogues of G.W.F. Hegel, and most specially in the ecstatic writings of the German Romantic poets: Johann Wolfgang von Goethe, Novalis, Heinrich Heine, Friedrich Schiller and Friedrich Hölderlin. Certainly Rilke was directly influenced by some of these writers and poets, and his poetry can be regarded as a development of German Romantic poetry.

Much has been made in Rilke criticism of the influence of the fervent Hellenism of Friedrich Hölderlin. Novalis seems to me just as significant, especially the Novalis of the aphorisms and philosophical fragments, such as:

> The world must be romanticized. (*Pollen*, 56)
> All must become nourishment. Art is to distill life form everything. To enliven all is the aim of life. (ib., 64)
> Transcendental poetry is an admixture of poetry and philosophy. (ib., 57)
> Everything can become magical-work. (ib, 73)
> All is seed (ib., 73)

RILKE

Transcendental poetry is as good a term as any for Rainer Maria Rilke's kind of poetry, and for Romantic poetry in general. In Novalis' exalted *Hymns To the Night*, we see the precursor of much of Rilke's ecstatic lyricism. Novalis' poetry is visionary, intense, idealized and idealizing. 'The poetic achievement is in the momentary glimpses of reality: what, in other contexts, we should call epiphanies', writes Glyn Tegai Hughes of Novalis [2].

Setting Rainer Maria Rilke within the German lyrical tradition – of Walter von der Vogelweide, Johannes Tauler, Angelus Silesius, Quirnus Kuhlmann, Johann Wolfgang von Goethe, Novalis, Friedrich Höldelrin, Theodor Storm, Friedrich Nietzsche, Heinrich Heine and Joseph von Eichendorff – emphasizes the meditative, intense nature of Rilke's poetry. Much of Rilke's œuvre is Romantic in temperament: the paganism, love of Hellenism, the invocation of old gods and goddesses, the fervour and tendency to extremism emotionally, the individualism, the pantheism and nature mysticism, the solitude, the Promethean rebellion, the belief in the magical qualities of poetry and art, the adherence to a bohemian, outsider lifestyle, the simultaneous rejection of establishment conservatism, the ontological restlessness, the epistemological uncertainty – all of these elements of Romanticism and many more are found in Rilke's work, and in much of twentieth century art.

In poems such as 'Declaration', from his *North Sea* cycle, Heinrich Heine depicts the archetypal poet of Romantic culture, alone on a windswept beach, musing on the nature of Nature:

> Shadowing downward came dusky evening,
>   Wildly the breakers rolled,
> I sat alone upon the shore and gazed
>   At the white dance of the waves.
>
> And my bosom heaved with the sea,
> A deep homesickness yearningly seized my heart
>   For thee, oh lovely image,

RILKE

> Who surround'st me everywhere,
> Who call'st to me everywhere,
> Everywhere, everywhere,
> In the rushing of the wind, in the dashing of the sea,
> And in the sighing of mine own breast.

This passage from the poems of Heinrich Heine is so typical of so much of Romantic poetry, whether it's by John Keats, William Wordsworth, Johann Wolfgang von Goethe, Alfred du Musset or Friedrich Hölderlin. Romanticism emphasizes the magic of art. Poetry is seen as a way of transforming reality and the self. The poet thus becomes what s/he always was, originally – the shaman, the dancing sorcerer, the one who can travel to other worlds and brings back news of what's happening there.

Rainer Maria Rilke is a shamanic poet, like Arthur Rimbaud, Robert Graves, Sappho, Francesco Petrarch, Walt Whitman and Novalis. Novalis said that 'the sorcerer is a poet... Poet and priest were in the beginning one' (1989, 33, 51). The shaman is the first artist: in the figure of the shaman, art and religion were united. Poetry originates in shamanism – this fact is authenticated by many commentators. [3] Of Novalis, Ronald Taylor wrote in *The Romantic Tradition In Germany:*

> His view of the poetic vocation, again like Hölderlin, lay in the phrase *poetas vates* – the poet as seer, as prophet – and presupposed the unity of poetry and religion. [4]

The poet is a magician, and Rainer Maria Rilke holds this view – as can be seen from many of his poems, such as 'The Goldsmith', 'Sorcery', 'Le Magicien', 'The Sorcerer' and 'The Spirit Ariel'. The latter poem stems from *The Tempest*. Rilke was fascinated by the figure of Prospero, the great Renaissance magus. A belief in the magical power of art to transform life lies at the heart of Rilke's poetry. Rilke called the god of poetry Apollo, and, later, Orpheus. The Angel, too, has many shamanic qualities.

RILKE

Rilke's poetic task is to become the shamanic artist, the Angel, Orpheus, Apollo, the poet who can make things really happen.

Poetry for Rainer Maria Rilke was a personal religion, as it was and is for many poets. Poetry was Rilke's way of dealing with the world, with life, and with his myriad feelings and experiences. Through poetry, Rilke could re-make the world in his own image. He is the god of his own poetry, as all poets are. He variously termed this god Apollo, the Angel or Orpheus, but these manifestations of mythic energies add up to the poet's self, the Rilke of the poems, the Rilke-poet.

What we see in the art of Rainer Maria Rilke is a poet following, as indulgently as he could, the trajectory of his inner, poetic life. Rilke appears as a 'pure poet' because he took his craft and vocation so seriously, and followed its journey with humility and diligence. Like Paul Valéry and Francesco Petrarch, Rilke produces what we can call 'pure poetry', an art which exists in and for itself, a poetry which aims at a purity that is both formal and philosophical, a poetry that aims for purity in language, expression, form, voice, tone, pattern, imagery, metaphor and message. (Other 'pure poets' would include Novalis, Gertrude Stein, Stéphane Mallarmé and Robert Graves).

This is the other side of Rainer Maria Rilke, the counterpart to the wild, romantic, Orphic mode of expression, which finds such a tumultuous expression in the Romantic poets. Rilke's formal influence is as much Charles Baudelaire as Johann von Goethe, as much the French poets of the 19th century as the German poets. In French artists such as Gustave Flaubert, Stendhal, Paul Verlaine, Stéphane Mallarmé and Paul Valéry, we find the aim of making language transparent; that is, the urge towards making it clearer and clearer, so that words themselves become transparent. Flaubert dreamt of a novel, like André Gide did, in which all of the extraneous detail has been boiled away, so that the essence remained. Stendhal spoke of making expression as simple and as clear as possible. One sees this aim fulfilling itself, in varying degrees of success, in the work of Gide, Valéry and Mallarmé.

In the poetry of the Symbolists, words themselves became objects: Paul Verlaine emphasized the musicality of words, while Stéphane Mallarmé used words as things in themselves, purified of all of their allusions, so that they became implements of pure expression. In Gertrude Stein's work, this tendency reaches its height. In Stein's superb poesie, linguistic communication is reduced to a vocabulary and syntax that is both minimal and powerfully expressive. Ludwig Wittgenstein said that the limits of his world were the same as the limits of his language: if questions can be put into words, so can the answers, he said; and, finally, Wittgenstein wrote that there are some things which cannot be said, and they are what is mystical. [5] These thoughts on language were echoed by Karl Kraus in his acerbic writings. But this zone, of darkness and silence where things cannot be said, is precisely where poets such as Rilke want to go. It is this zone that they try to suggest, describe or point towards.

One way of reaching this beyond-language zone is by exploding language in cascades of words, as James Joyce did. Rainer Maria Rilke's way is more that of Joyce's disciple, Samuel Beckett, who reduced, like Gertrude Stein, his vocabulary and presentation so much that it became mystical. Rainer Maria Rilke is not as ruthless as Beckett, but he does, like Paul Valéry, believe in his mysticality of language, a mysticality which, as Valéry noted, Stéphane Mallarmé had introduced into poetry.

Rainer Maria Rilke is a poet of the invisible. What he's trying to get at is invisible, unknown, unseen, unfelt, dark, yet always there. The German Expressionist painter Max Beckmann spoke of trying to make the invisible visible, and Rilke's aim is, similarly, to reify, magnify and make manifest the secret feelings, the inner essences, the unseen realities of life. The British poet Peter Redgrove spoke of authentic things beings both strange and commonplace: this is precisely Rilke's area of poetic operation: not a fantastic, other-worldly zone, but a place right in the midst of life. Redgrove talked of the poet trying to forge a pathway to the strange and everyday things, so that the reader can make their own way to them. Rilke has a similar quest.

The quest is alchemical, mythical, psychological, præternatural, as well as poetic. The battleground is the poetic self. 'I have an inner self of which I was ignorant,' says the alienated narrator of *Malte Laurids Brigge* (14-15). Rilke's quest is for Jungian integration and individuation, a quest for wholeness, unity in life: this ontological unity is the same as the poetic/ artistic unity. Rilke is the poet of inner spaces, of inside worlds. Like Stéphane Mallarmé and Paul Valéry, Rilke is a precise poet, dreaming of the perfect form for the perfect poetic expression. Few poets are as exact. It is Rilke's poetic brilliance that makes him so highly regarded, not simply his mysticism. 'Rarely has a European poet stirred so many minds and inspired so many pens', noted F.W. von Heerikhuizen, and the reason must surely be due to Rilke's talent as a poet, rather than as a mystic (altho' the two are inseparable). As Frank Wood put it in his excellent biography: 'the craft aspect of his work, the creativity of the "word", is the very key to his æsthetic, thought, and "message"' (218).

Rainer Maria Rilke's poetry is marked by lucidity, passion, distance, synæsthesia, ambivalence, openness, elegance and magic. Though his forms are meticulously worked out, he describes violent and disturbing states of consciousness, which slip into magic on the one side, and into self-regard on the other. Like contemporary novelists such as J.G. Ballard and Ursula Le Guin, Rilke tries to depict the inner spaces that no one thought existed. Rilke shows that they exist, and in the everyday world. In his poems he asks questions such as, 'have you ever really looked at a bowl of roses before?', or 'looked at that archway over there?' Rilke shows those things as if they were new.

RILKE

Rainer Maria Rilke's poetry looks forward to the Surrealist artists, to André Breton's automatic writing, to Yves Tanguy's painted dreamscapes, or Max Ernst's fantasies. But Rilke's inner world is deeper than that of Surrealism. Despite his great emphasis on the visual sense, Rilke's world is beyond and below it – more like the dark world of touch in the art of D.H. Lawrence (in Lawrence's short stories such as *The Blind Man*). It is a world of super-sense, the sixth sense, the occult faculties that everyone possesses but that society suppresses.

Like Arthur Rimbaud, Rainer Maria Rilke tries to reach this strange/ commonplace realm. Hence his use of the Angel, or the 'thingness' of the *New Poems* (1908). The *Duino Elegies* are full of marvellous passages, but the work aims beyond the usual five senses. Like Rimbaud, Rilke is a supremely synæsthetic poet. This comes, formally, from Symbolist poetry, from the emphasis in the work of Paul Verlaine and Stéphane Mallarmé on the materiality, musicality and thingness of words. Rilke says similar things about words in his essay "Primal Sound". He claims that modern, European poetry over-emphasizes the visual sense and neglects the others: he advocates a multi-sensory poetic experience:

> the finished poem can come about only on condition that the world, simultaneously grasped by these five levers [the senses], appear under a given aspect upon that supernatural plane which is precisely the plane of poetry. (In H. Bloch, 50).

What Rainer Maria Rilke does is to take the emphasis on the materiality of the word and develop it far beyond the modernist poetics of T.S. Eliot and Ezra Pound. Rilke's creative technique was to work from within – in life and in poetry. In Rilkean poetics, poetic language must be made full and rich, but without being over-indulgent, or pretentious. 'A poem enters into language from within,' asserted Rilke, 'in an aspect forever averted from us. It fills the language wondrously, rising to its very brim – but it never again thrusts towards us' (LB, 51).

This is the feeling we get from Rainer Maria Rilke's poems, as from all great poems, whether they are by John Skelton, Matsuo Basho, Rabindranath Tagore or George Seferis – a sense of fullness, completeness and richness, where the poem has been filled up to the brim, like a glass of water, but nothing spills out – the water rests quivering inside the container, the meniscus poised to break, poised to flood.

Rainer Maria Rilke's poems operate at this point of balance between openness and closure, between centripedal and centrifugal motion, between the poem being all symbol and being all object bereft of symbolism, allusion and mythology. It is the inwardness of poetry that Rilke develops so successfully. In this view, he is the apotheosis of that self-referential poetics which was begun in the poesie of Charles Baudelaire and refined in the work of Stéphane Mallarmé. There is no conflict, then, between Rilke's 'in-seeing' of the *Neue Gedichte* period and the Orphic philosophy of the mature works. Rilke's poems are created from the inside outwards, as H.E. Holthusen noted in his biography:

> In Rilke's Orphic language the idea of a magic world of metamorphoses in space is realized... The syntax is made to express not logical sequence in time, but magical identification in space. The poem does not develop in an outward direction, but like an ornament, 'decoratively', into itself. (35, 40)

Rainer Maria Rilke's is a poetry of essences, but he suggested essences not through presence but through absence. Sometimes, he would like to get rid of the poet her/ himself – 'to write as though one were – nobody', he said in 1925. [7] Absence is crucial in Rilke's art, as it is in Samuel Beckett's art. Rilke's poetry is rich in the sense that the poetry of William Wordsworth or Arthur Rimbaud is rich; his is not a poetry of incidents, images, meanderings, and over-abundance. Like Paul Valéry and Stéphane Mallarmé, Rilke squeezes and squeezes language until only the essence, or the absence shadowing the essence, is left.

Rainer Maria Rilke is something of an abstract artist. The black painted squares of Kasimir Malevich suggest, like Rilke's poetic roses, the Madonna, and divinity, but in an oblique manner. The connections are there, for those willing (or ready) to make them. Rilke's poetry demands a thoughtful, careful reader. His poetry asks to be devoured slowly, circumspectly, phrase by phrase. One cannot rush reading Rilke's work – nor any poetry of this kind, for that matter. The experiences Rilke aims to locate are delicate and easily damaged by rushing in too swiftly. The reader has to keep focussed.

Rainer Maria Rilke's is a suggestive poetry, like Symbolist poetry. He hints rather than shouts, and a silence runs throughout his poetry (as with Samuel Beckett). With a few delicate brush-marks the Chinese landscape painter depicts a tree, a mountain, a cloud. Similarly with Rilke. His poetry is compressed, like that of Francesco Petrarch or Paul Valéry, and is sparing in its imagery. One thinks of *haiku* poetry, the Japanese form of short lyrics. The seventeen-syllable *haiku* lyric, like the Greek epigram, is life compressed, an emblematic, economical distillation of life. Masters such as Matsuo Basho and Yosa Buson (from the 17th century) suggested vast spaces using a minimum of words:

> Wind in the West
> fallen leaves
> gathering in the East.
> (Yosa Buson) [8]

> Journey's end –
> still alive
> this autumn evening.
> (Matsuo Basho) [9]

RILKE

Haiku poetry targets a space that is both commonplace and strange, the spiritual zone of authentic art. While the philosophical background to Rainer Maria Rilke's poetry is different from that of the *haiku* of Basho and Buson, his poems produce similar responses. Rilke's poems provoke a feeling of mystery and wonder. His poems possess that enigmatic quality of *haiku*, which can so suddenly and completely evoke an atmosphere, a feeling, an experience, a memory, a dream. As an example of Rilke's ability to create 'pure poetry', this is the poem 'Nacht. Oh du in Tiefe gelöstes' ('Night. O face against my face') of 1924:

>Nacht. Oh du in Tiefe gelöstes
>Gesicht an meinem Gesicht.
>Du, meines staunenden Anschauns größtes
>Übergewicht.
>
>Nacht, in meinem Blicke erschauernd,
>aber in sich so fest;
>unerschöpfliche Schöpfung, dauernd
>über dem Erdenrest;
>
>voll von jungen Gestirnen, die Feuer
>aus der Flucht ihres Saums
>schleudern ins lautlose Abenteuer
>des Zwischenraums:
>
>wie, durch dein bloßes Dasein, erschein ich,
>Übertrefferin, klein –;
>doch, mit der dunkelen Erde einig,
>wag ich es, in dir zu sein.
>
>(Night. O face against my face
>dissolved into deepness.
>You my marvelling look's most immense
>preponderance.
>
>Night, in my gaze a spasm,
>in yourself made so fast;
>inexhaustible genesis, outlasting

RILKE

earthly remains;

full of young planets that hurl
fire from the flight of their seams
into the soundless adventure
of the space between:

by your mere existence, exceeder,
how small I grow –;
but at one with the darkened earth
I dare be in you.)
(Tr. Michael Hamburger from *Dance the Orange*)

Rainer Maria Rilke is a restrained, refined poet, who only occasionally allows himself an outburst of uncontrolled passion (as in the *Duino Elegies*). Rilke's Angel, for instance, is not a rich profusion of feathers, gold, light and sensual resplendence, as it might be in the work of Charles Baudelaire or Walt Whitman. Rilke's Angel is instead hinted at, not fully fleshed out, a feeling or an experience, an abstract thought.

Rainer Maria Rilke's poetic voice is quiet, contemplative, musical, complex, lucid, and at times passionate. Sometimes, his Orphic voice can become strident, but it is usually hypnotic, seductive, beautiful. One quickly becomes entranced by Rilke's flowing words, as one is mesmerized by Sappho or Arnaut Daniel. Like all true poets, Rilke can weave a magic spell about the reader/ listener. There are certain poets who can make magic instantly, within a few words of a poem. We might suggest poets such as William Shakespeare, Sappho, Arthur Rimbaud, Francesco Petrarch and Pablo Neruda. These are poets in whom Orpheus lives and breathes with the fervour of pure, passionate poetry.

Of the shamanic poet-god Orpheus, Mircea Eliade wrote in his study of shamanism:

As to Orpheus, his myth displays several elements that can be compared to the shamanic ideology and technique. The most significant is, of course, his descent to Hades to bring back the soul of his wife, Eurydice... Orpheus also displays other characteristics of a "Great Shaman": his healing art, his love for music and animals, his "charms", his power of divination. Even his character of "culture hero" is not in contradiction to the best shamanic tradition – was not the "first shaman" the messenger sent by God to defend humanity against diseases and to civilize it? A final detail of the Orpheus myth is clearly shamanic. Cut off by the bacchantes and thrown into the Gebrus, Orpheus' head floated to Lesbos, singing. It later served as an oracle. [10]

The poet is an artist of both worlds – the upper and the lower, Earth and the Underworld. The poet moves between these worlds. Like Dionysis, who was also torn to shreds by wild mænads, Orpheus is a god of death and resurrection. He is constantly giving birth to himself. Such a god would naturally endear themselves, to a poet such as Rilke who, like D.H. Lawrence, aches for rebirth. In the Orpheus myth of Ancient Greece, Rilke sees parallels with the poet's experience of transforming life through poetry. Orpheus sings the world into existence, in much the same way that the Bushmen and aborigines of Australia sing of the *alchuringa* mythic dreamtime.

For poets such as Rainer Maria Rilke, Francesco Petrarch and Arthur Rimbaud, poetry is magical transformation, literally and physically as well as symbolically and psychologically. Robert Graves said the poem was a magic circle. Inside the circle, the spell starts weaving its enchantment. In Rilke's art, as in poets such as Rimbaud and William Shakespeare, one sees a rejuvenation of poetry, from its shamanic roots upwards. The tree of Orphic poetry is revitalized by a passionate song. One sees Rilke breaking into a new phase of poetry creativity – with the *New Poems*, then the *Duino Elegies*, then once more, in the *Sonnets To Orpheus*. Each phase is a breakthrough: one feels the excitement in the poems, as they arrive, as with Rimbaud's discoveries of

RILKE

poetic form and fervour. The *Duino Elegies* were written over ten or so years, while the *Sonnets To Orpheus* were composed in a matter of days, in a flood of creative endeavour. Both are whirlwinds of poetic energy. The *Sonnets To Orpheus* open on a high point no less startling than the famous cry at the beginning of the 'First Elegy':

> A tree ascended there. Oh pure transcendence!
> Oh Orpheus sings! Oh tall tree in the ear!
> And all things hushed. Yet even in that silence
> A new beginning, beckoning, change appeared. (Mit, 237)

Rainer Maria Rilke's Orpheus takes us back to Friedrich Nietzsche's deity Dionysis. The wild, free spirit of Nietzsche's Dionysis is counterpointed by the rationalism of Apollo. For poets, such as Francesco Petrarch, Apollo is the god of poetry as much as Dionysis. But whether the god of poesie is Apollo, Orpheus or Dionysis, or Muses such as Aphrodite, Isis, Diana or the Virgin Mary, the point is the mythical dimension which is invoked and reborn every time a deity of poetry is called upon and used in the act of making poetry.

There is a tendency in Rainer Maria Rilke's work to go wild in the Nietzschean fashion – without this wildness, the *Duino Elegies* would be quite different. The energy comes from pure lyricism, which is not simply joy, but a way of making the experience of life deeper, richer, more luminous, more piercing, more tragic. Friedrich Nietzsche described this psychological deepening of experience in his 'Das trunken Lied' ('The Songs of Ecstasy'):

> the world is deep and deeper than day ever conceived. Its pain is deep – joy deeper even that heart's grief! Pain says: Pass away; but all joy seeks eternity – seeks deep, deep eternity. (L. Forster, 375)

Joy was the goal of much of Friedrich Nietzsche's Dionysian

philosophy, as it was for André Gide and Rainer Maria Rilke, two artists influenced by Nietzsche. In books such as *Fruits of the Earth* and *The Immoralist*, Gide argued for a philosophy of life based on joy – but a joy, as in the philosophy of Arthur Schopenhauer, gained thru opening oneself up existentially to *everything* life offers, pain as much as pleasure. In his *Sonnets To Orpheus*, Rilke presents us with a life-philosophy of acceptance and generosity, one built on praise rather than negation. In the *Sonnets To Orpheus*, Rilke tempers his Nietzschean ecstasy, which is at times so fierce ('Shatter me music, with rhythmical fury!' he writes [11]), and embraced lamentation as much as joy. The result is an Orphic lyricism which echoes as closely as possible the spirit of life, and in doing so helps to transform it.

As Edith Sitwell explained in her essential book *The Orphic Voice*, the Orphic poet should not simply go crazy in a quasi-Nietzschean manner, but, rather, the Orphic poet should focus his/ her energies on making poetry:

> An Orphic lyricist is not a gusher of imagery and sentiments. What it does mean is that he must do his thinking strictly in lyric, in concentratedly poetic, postlogical, mythological terms. It is at this exact point that Orpheus and Rilke meet and soar together. (376-7)

In Rainer Maria Rilke's art, shamanic madness is carefully controlled; yet, at the same time, Rilke lets himself go. He is a very free poet, in that he writes a lot of poetry, and he writes a lot of letters, and he lets it all flow out of him. Rilke's sense of form, shape, language, stanza, rhyme, meaning and metaphor is highly pronounced – he is one of the most lyrical of lyrical poets. Yet it seems to come naturally to him, and he seems to write easily, freely, openly. One image of Rilke, during the time of the *New Poems*, is when he sat in the Jardins des Planes, or the Louvre Museum, waiting for the thingness of the object of his intense contemplation to show itself. Rilke often speaks of waiting, of the importance of waiting – rather as a painter will speak of waiting for the right moment in which to create. But the other Rilke is someone who can create easily. He said he didn't need drugs, Muses, or any kind of stimulants to work himself up to writing. 'Language is a perpetual Orphic song', said Percy Bysshe Shelley in *Prometheus Unbound*; for Rilke, writing itself, whether letters or poems, could be a perpetual song of Orpheus. Rilke's goals of unity and fulfilment are possible only, perhaps, in art, in writing, in the Orphic song.

In D.H. Lawrence's 1916 novel *The Rainbow*, which Rainer Maria Rilke read and was affected by, [12] Ursula Brangwen talks of the wild darkness that surrounds us: what Rilke's poetry does is to throw firebrands out into the darkness to illuminate it for a while. For a moments, the dark unconscious is lit up, exposed, highlighted. This is what poetry-as-shamanism does, opening up deep, neglected realms of experience. No wonder that Rilke's poetry (and that of others) is deemed opaque, difficult, or obscure; it is also electric, erotic, and hypnotic. When you take off your shoes in Summer and feel again as if for the first time the cool grass or the wet sand – this is what poetry can do.

Like Sappho, Friedrich Hölderlin or John Keats, Rainer Maria Rilke can kick up a Promethean fireball of poetry in which revelation is uppermost, and the crags and crevices of the unconscious, like some kind of black sea floor, are lit up: like a Freudian psychiatrist, Rilke uncovers the unconscious, but because poetry is his instrument of dissection, he covers his tracks, remains ambiguous, and dives back into the sea of the unconscious. Ambiguity is always maintained, even in the most lucid utterances. So one never knows for certain what the Rilke-poet is saying. Rilke, like all poets, retains his shamanic shape-changing ability. We would not wish him to made crudely plain statements – he might as well write a car manual.

Like his Angel, Rainer Maria Rilke moves between light and

dark, sensual and supra-sensual, ecstasy and despair, eroticism and detachment. His Gnostic duality is not a simply moral dichotomy of good versus evil, but of clarity versus opacity, the visible against the invisible. The unification that Rilke (and all poets) is trying to achieve is not easy. Much has to die in order to make the poetic unity live. André Gide spoke of the need for the seed to die so that it may bear fruit. For Gide, the moral precepts of Jesus were æsthetic as well as ontological. Novalis went further, and said that, 'all is seed' (*Pollen*, 73): in other words, nothing is wasted, for the artist, and everything can be useful, can give birth to something. The fruitfulness of life is a notion one finds in writers such as Henry Miller, D.H. Lawrence and Anaïs Nin. The view is simply that nothing is lost or wasted for the artist, the transformer of the stuff of life, is able to transmute loss and waste into something rich and strange.

•

It might be useful at the point to look at some of Rainer Maria Rilke's poetry, in order to see why he is probably the greatest lyrical poet of the 20th century (a lyrical poet, not a love poet). Rilke's lyricism soars above most other poets of the 20th century. The typical study of Rilke's work begins with the early poems, moves thru the *Neue Gedichte*, to the *Duino Elegies* and finally to the *Sonnette an Orpheus* and the *Late Poems*. We begin with the *Sonnets To Orpheus,* as they embody Rilke's mature poetic views and creations, and shed light on all of Rilke's movement towards a free-flowing, open but stylized Orphic lyricism.

Before quoting from Rainer Maria Rilke's poetry, we must again remind ourselves of the inadequacy of translating Rilke. It doesn't help much having the original German printed beside the translation (if you can't read German). Only the original German as Rilke wrote it will do. Translation alters so much, yet it has to be done, and if we are to get close to Rilke's art, we will simply have to include the translations.

RILKE

For the moment, we will print Rainer Maria Rilke's original texts, as well as a translation, from poem II, no. 4, of the *Sonnette an Orpheus* (1922):

O dieses ist das Tier, das nicht giebt.
Sie wußtens nicht und habens jeden Falls
– sein Wandeln, seine haltung, seinen Hals,
bis in des stillen Blickes Licht – geliebt.

Zwar *war* es nicht. Doch weil sie's liebten, ward
ein reines Tier. Sie ließen immer Raum.
Und in dem Raume, klar und ausgespart,
erhob es leicht sein Haupt und brachte kaum

zu sein. Sie nährten es mit keinem Korn,
nur immer mit der Möglichkeit, es sei.
Und die gab solche Stärke an das tier,

daß es aus sich ein Stirnhorn trieb. Ein Horn.
Zu einer Jungfrau kam es weiß herbei –
und war im Silber-Spiegel und in ihr.

(This is the non-existent animal.
Not knowing that, they loved it, loved its ways,
its neck, its posture, loved its quiet gaze
down to the light within it, loved it all.

True, it was *not*. But, because loved, a pure
beast came to be. A space was kept, conceded.
And in that space, left blank for it, secure,
it gently raised its head and hardly needed

to be. They fed it on no kind of corn,
but always only with the right to be.
And on the beast such power this could confer,

its brow put forth new growth. A single horn.
White, it sought out a virgin's company –
and was inside the mirror and in her.)
(Trans. Michael Hamburger, *Dance the Orange*)

RILKE

Each poet invents poetic forms anew, and Rainer Maria Rilke reclaims the sonnet form from its traditional use in love poetry. Rilke's sonnets have nothing to do with the Elizabethan/Renaissance love sonnet sequences, but they do have some of the qualities of the sonnets of Dante Alighieri and Francesco Petrarch, which meditate on the same issues time after time (Rilke was part of a cultural trend in modernist poetry for taking up mediæval and Renaissance poetic forms). Rilke takes the sonnet form and, like Petrarch, bends it into all sorts of shapes, makes it do all kinds of things. He will, like William Shakespeare, construct sonnets from one sentence, with many clauses and sections; or he will, like Charles Baudelaire, create a series of short, punchy phrases which shatter the wholeness of each line. Rilke's sonnets do not follow the old rules of splitting the sonnet into an octave and a sestet, but create their own formal patterns. Rilke does stick to one very important tradition in poetry: the rhyme, which plays a key role in Rilke's lyricism (and is partly why Rilke is so difficult to translate (following a rhyme scheme forces translators into awkward phrases and sentences).

The sonnet is attractive because of its symmetry, its shape, its compressed form, its length and its layout which seems well-suited to a meditation on big issues, like love, death, war, loss, and being. The sonnet is one of the great forms of pure lyrical poetry. The sonnet demands much of the poet: the poet has to work hard to produce a decent sonnet (try it – it's a superb exercise for poets).

This is the last poem in *Sonnets To Orpheus*, II. 29:

> Stiller Freund der vielen Fernen, fühle
> wie dein Atem noch den Raum vermehrt.
> Im Gebälk der finstern Glockenstühle
> lass dich läuten. Des, was an dir zehrt,
>
> wird ein Starkes über dieser Nahrung,
> Geh in der Verwandlung aus und ein.

RILKE

Vas ist deine leidendste Erfahrung?
Ist dir trinken bitter, werde Wein,

Sei in dieser Nacht aus Übermass
Zauberkraft am Kreuzweg deiner Sinne,
ihrer seitsamen Begegnung Sinn.

Und wenn dich das Irdische vergass,
zu der stillen Erde sag: Ich rinne.
Zu dem raschen Wasser sprich: Ich bin.

(Still friend of many silent spaces, feel how your short breath enlarges even space. In beams of gloomy belfries be a bell, let yourself peal. What has you in embrace will grow a strong force from such nourishment. End and begin in utter transformation. Tell me what your greatest suffering meant. If drinking's bitter, then turn into wine. And in this night beyond all our conjecture be magical where all your senses grow, be the whole point of their unique encounter. And when what's earthly has forgotten you, say this to the silent earth: I flow. Speak to the rolling water: I endure.
(Mit, 255; SO/N, 145; Les, 58; SO/N, 56)

In this sonnet, Rainer Maria Rilke packs in a lot: the connection between breath, space, night and presence; transformation; loss; suffering; sensuality; mystery and magic, personifications (of the earth, water, wine, the night, etc); philosophy ('I am'); use of the senses (sound: ringing out like a bell; taste: drinking and wine; sight: the night, and so on). In the sonnet, Rilke suggests many of his preoccupations: the importance of transformation; the significance, and the sensual experience, of night, of massive space; the magic of the night-enclosed senses; the use of Biblical imagery and metaphors (changing oneself into wine); the proud, Nietzschean affirmation: 'I am'; the presence of essence through absence.

As in many poets, Rainer Maria Rilke's early work is often mannered, precious, embarrassingly self-conscious, derivative, trite and banal. The early works include: *The Book of Hours, The Book of Pictures, Tales of God, Visions of Christ, Coronet* and *In My*

RILKE

Honour. A pious preciousness is found in many young artists (from Early Renaissance painters (such as Fra Filippo Lippi) to the latest pop idols.) Rilke's early poetry is part of *fin-de-siècle* decadence, Pre-Raphaelite decorative mediævalism, and the fashionable, effete æstheticism of J.-K. Huysmans (in *Against Nature*), Pierre Louÿs, Walter Pater, Aubrey Beardsley and Oscar Wilde. Rilke retained a Middle Ages flavour in his poetry up to the last works – a mediævalism of innocence and religious faith such as that which informs the altarpieces of Fra Angelico, say, or the romance works of Chrétien de Troyes. Even in his late pieces, Rilke has that faith in transformation which seems as much mediæval as Nietzschean – a certain stoicism which looks death in the face and doesn't blench.

Rainer Maria Rilke's poetic style is economical – he uses the same words again and again: *Dasein, Tod, Raum, Stille, Nacht*. The repeated use of the same terms, the same forms and shapes, the same subjects, is all a way of getting closer to the goal, the aim, the essence of whatever it is the artist is trying to reach. One sees painters using the same colours, the same gestures and tones, the same textures, glazes, forms and structures. Painters of this kind, who keep hacking away at the same scene or motif, include Vincent van Gogh, J.M.W. Turner, Mark Rothko and Ad Reinhardt. Thus, though there are many differences between Rilke's early and late poetry, the same atmospheres appear (hushed solitude, in a room or in a landscape), the same religious imagery (angels, gods, etc), the same flowers (roses), the same darkness and the night, the same use of animals, objects and mythical characters, the same self-referentiality, the same Biblical allusions, the same distrust of erotic love, and the same sense of death.

Rainer Maria Rilke's poetic voice, which is a large part of a poet's personal mark, is both coolly dispassionate and crazily, swooningly involved; it is a voice that is at times a distant, privileged observer, and a voice of someone embroiled in life; it is a voice capable of convoluted sentences and compact, terse phrases; it is the voice of a poetic self at once wildly, painfully confused and proudly authoritative; it is a voice of someone sexless, genderless, bodiless, yet also heavily involved with its subjects. Rilke's poems are constructed out of invisible, angelic word-stuff, something like ectoplasm which the poet shapes, magically, like Prospero the magician, into a formally precise poem. The space of Rilke's poems is hard to define. He does not site the action of his poems in the everyday world. He does not offer easily recognizable references – to people, places, history, politics. There is no particular time zone for a Rilke poem. Rilke is not concerned with history or his society in a direct way. He alludes to socio-historical events in an oblique manner. His poems operate in a mythic space, a timeless space, a poet's place – this is the poetic realm of C.P. Cavafy, Paul Verlaine, Fyodor Tyutchev, and Catullus. It is the magic circle which the poet creates, as Robert Graves said. Poetic language produces the space, and the poet invites the reader to enter it. The act of reading/ listening is one of complicity: reader and poet agree to work up the magic.

It is this poetic space of the poem, a combination of poetic voice, syntax, vocabulary, word order, allusion, metaphor, narrative, imagery, synæsthesia, meaning, music, context and shape, that is what fascinates us about a poem. It is this magic space that we enter when consuming a poem, and the magic space is instantly recognizable when we read, say, Dante Alighieri or Antonio Machado or Elizabeth Browning.

Rainer Maria Rilke's poetic space is vividly apparent in the two poems we have already quoted in full. Rilke's style is something limpid, lucid, simple but intricate, clear but multi-allusive, like Paul Valéry at his best, or Arthur Rimbaud when he's not imploding too quickly like a supernova star. Of course, Rilke's style (his poetic voice and space), sometimes backfires and becomes mere mouthing of platitudes, or repetitive banalities, or it sinks into an over-elaborate, over-paradoxical, over-enriched swamp, or the repetition of key words makes them reach saturation point, semantically, and the meaning is confused or slips away. In Francesco Petrarch's poetry and that of the troubadours, the word *amor* (love) soon loses its impact, because it's so over-used. Similarly, Rilkean words such as *dasein* are forced to carry so much of what the Rilke-poet is trying to achieve. The problem is that poets have special, magical words, which they employ time after time, in a variety of ways and contexts. The reader has to be aware of the multiple meanings of the treasured words. Examples might include *laurel* in Petrarch's *œuvre*, which connotes, among other things, Laura, the beloved, the myth of Daphne and Apollo, poetry itself, and poetic immortality. Robert Graves uses the word 'black' in a special way, meaning the unknown/ unseen faculties which we posses, and also the Black Goddess, who presides over this miraculous realm of experience (which corresponds to Rilke's synæsthetic open spaces). Graves's 'black' is the opposite of William Shakespeare's use of the word 'black' in the *Sonnets*, while 'black' in contemporary politics has a whole new set of meanings and uses.

In Rainer Maria Rilke's work, words such as *dasein* are crucial: the word in the famous phrase in sonnet 1.3, 'Gesang ist Dasein' ('Song is existence'), in the *Sonnets To Orpheus*. Rilke's poetry, for good or ill, pivots around the concept of being. For him, it is the highest of all verbs: 'to be', and the precept of most of his poetry is, simply, *be*. That is, one must *be* before and after everything else. This is the meaning of the *Sonnets To Orpheus,* and much of the rest of the poetry. While other poets might regarded the verb 'to love' as the holiest and most noble of all verbs, Rilke sees the verb 'to be' as the most sacred. In this he is like Arthur Rimbaud, Walt Whitman, Novalis and Gertrude Stein. These are poets who asserted their artistic independence fiercely. They are individualists, whose poetry is idiosyncratic, self-aware and powerful. There is no one else quite like Rimbaud, or Robert Herrick, or Sappho.

In Rainer Maria Rilke's art, the assertion of autonomy, of beingness, of sovereignty, is part of his cool but passionate, clear but opaque, simple but intricate lyricism. This strongly-affirmed æsthetic independence is founded in his concept of *ding*, or thingness, where the flowers, gazelles and other things exist in their own right, within their own space, just as Rilke wished his poems to do. The animals or things are not simply *there*, and neither are the poems, or the words within the poems. Rather, they exude beingness: they *are*, in a self-aware, simple fashion. The things, animals and poems cast a magic space around themselves: Rilke spoke in a similar way of words collecting poetic meanings around themselves, so they are word clusters, like star clusters – constellations of meaning. [13]

TWO

SPACE

Angels' loving is space.
World-space is like the perceiving
of loving angels. All
filled with their starry gift.

Rainer Maria Rilke, untitled poem, Feb 9, 1922 (P/ 26, 271)

Rainer Maria Rilke's poetic province is a wild, breathless space. For him, the notion of space is central. He calls it space, or the Open, or the Night, or the stars, or world-space, or the void, and so on. The prime poetic place of Rilke's poetry is a vast, dark space: the starry night, which features in so many poems, is the outward manifestation of the huge inner spaces of the poet. It is both an abstract space, the space of art, of the art object, of an imaginary picture plane upon which he paints his feelings, as well as a real space which exists for the poet and which he creates around himself when he is making poetry.

Rainer Maria Rilke's poetic space is an artistic creation which becomes the basis for a philosophy of life. The infinite, black space is where Rilke the poet (or his soul) would like to live. He is not terrified of space, as Kit is in *The Sheltering Sky* by Paul Bowles: beyond the sheltering sky is a chaotic void; but Rilke embraces such violent darkness. The void in Bowles' novel is full of the terror of meaninglessness, what Mircea Eliade called the 'terror of history', which follows on from the pessimism of a worldview based on Albert Einstein's Second Law of Thermodynamics. In this post-Einsteinian view, there is nothing one can do to stop the cosmic decay – everything is inevitable – one must sit back and watch it all collapse. This theory, called chaos theory these days, is embraced by Rilke, for he affirms the importance of death. Further, Rilke's talk of seeds and growth echoes André Gide's notion that the seed must die in order to bear fruit.

Rainer Maria Rilke's poetic space is full of death, but it is also a womb at the same time. The seed dies but bears fruit: this simple idea is also the most profound, and one must grasp it fully to understand what the evanescent thing called 'life' is. Rilke realized, as do many poets, that death is all around us all the time. We move in landscape full of ghosts. Poets like to commune with these ghosts (one thinks of poets such as C.P. Cavafy, Thomas Hardy, Percy Shelley and Francesco Petrarch – poets for whom the past was vividly, palpably alive).

Rainer Maria Rilke's dwelling on death is nothing unusual for a poet working in a religion which is profoundly death-conscious, which exalts the moment of death time and time again with its endless depictions of Christ dying on the Cross. The Crucifixion, not the Ascension, is the central image of Western, Christian religion. The usual way that artists integrate death into their works is to say, typically, how close love is to death, or how death is the great conclusion of a grand passion, or that sex and death are fused in love, or that death is the gateway to a higher life (in Heaven). All of these views are expressed in Western authors – in the work of Dante Alighieri, Ovid, William Shakespeare, the Marquis de Sade, Charles Baudelaire, Thomas Mann and Knut Hamsun.

Rainer Maria Rilke's death-awareness is a little different from the usual, Occidental (masculine) notions: death is very close, says Rilke; so close that life becomes one with it (in the *Duino Elegies*, Mit, 316). For Rilke, death is the side or face of life that is turned away from us, [1] and we must look at it. One must become fully associated with death. The senses must be made fully death-conscious. One must stare straight into the face of death, just as the Rilke-poet does in Rilke's 'Requiem For a Friend' (Paula Modersohn-Becker):

> Come into the candlelight. I'm not afraid
> to look the dead in the face. When they return,
> they have a right, as much as other Things do,
> to pause and refresh themselves within our vision. (Mit, 77)

The poetic requiems show Rainer Maria Rilke at his most lyrical, fluid and acute: the openness of the requiem or elegy form allows his concept of openness to expand as much as he can make it expand. The 'Open', as it appears in the 'Eighth Elegy', is a special kind of awareness of death which sites a living thing firmly with-the-world. Humans, says Rilke, are too aware of death: animals and plants and things go into it, become one with it. There is always something in the way for us, Rilke claims, so that lovers are close, but the beloved 'blocks the view'. What Rilke wants is to live in the Open without second thoughts, doubts or desire:

> Never, not for single day, do we have
> before us that pure space into which flowers
> endlessly open. (Mit, 193)

Death makes humans see objects as opaque, while Rainer

RILKE

Maria Rilke would prefer to make all things transparent. Here his notion of death concords with Oriental mysticism, with, for instance, Tibetan Buddhism, which speaks of the 'Clear Light of the Void'. The urge to make language (communication) transparent, a goal of poets such as Paul Valéry, is part of Rilke's notion of transparency-through-death-awareness. The two – art and life – are the same in Rilke's poetics, so art and death are fused, too. Art thus helps the artist to embrace death. And this is precisely what Rilke does in so many poems – he embraces death and exploits its possibilities. Thus we read of people and animals and objects that 'blossom' in death. The ripening that Rilke discusses in the *Sonnets To Orpheus* and the *Duino Elegies* comes as much from death as from life. In a letter of 1925, Rilke explains: 'when a tree blossoms, death as well as life blossoms in it, and the field is full of death, which from its reclining face sends for a rich expression of life'. [2] This has affinities with the Japanese concept of *mono no aware* or transience, impermanence, as manifested in the national symbol of Japan, cherry blossom.

In Rainer Maria Rilke's poetics, to focus upon death is not to focus upon decay and failure in a morbid fashion, as might be supposed, but to concentrate all the more intensely on life, on living life, on experiencing life as fully as possible. Denying death, Rilke argues, helps to deny life. So the notion of blossoming in death is central to Rilke, and is found in so many of his poems, not just in the requiems (tho' in those poems death at least has a prime position, philosophically and formally). In Rilke's 'Requiem For Wolf Graf von Kalckreuth', we read:

> If only, dissolved in a stream of melancholy
> and overcome, only half conscious,
> in motion round the distant stars,
> you would find the joy you misplaced here,
> pushed into the deadness of your dreams.
> How close you came to it here, my dear. (RBR, 47)

RILKE

Rainer Maria Rilke wishes to turn the transcendence in death of Christianity into a transformation through immanence, a death-consciousness such as is found in Gnosticism, and Tantric sex magic. In a key letter of 1923, Rilke explained his concept of death:

> I am not saying that we should love death, but we should love life so generously, so without calculation and selection, that we involuntarily come to include, and to love, death too (life's averted half)... It is a friend, our deepest friend... Life simultaneously says Yes and No. Death (I implore you to believe this!) is the true Yes-sayer. It says *only* Yes. In the presence of eternity. [3]

The emphasis on death in Rainer Maria Rilke's poetic philosophy (which caused Princess Marie to call him a poet of death), is only part of Rilke's urge towards a philosophy of life based on acceptance and beingness. Death is not only a friend, Rilke insists, but an 'intimate companion' (*Duino Elegies*, Mit, 203). When death is anthropomorphized in this intimate fashion, death becomes something of a lover – quite different from the traditional Grim Reaper, the gaunt figure in black robes holding a scythe. When Rilke addresses Paula Modorsohn-Becker in his requiem poem for her, he addresses her as the embodiment of death, as an actual person he once knew, and as the abstract but for him so real feeling which can help him live better:

> Are you still there? Still hiding in some corner?
> ...If you're still there, if there is still some place
> within this darkness where your spirit vibrates
> sensitively to and fro on the shallow sound waves
> that a voice, lonely in the lonely night,
> excites in the air-stream of a lofty room:
> hear me and help me... (LP, 102)

Rainer Maria Rilke does not deny that life is painful – 'isn't life itself dreadful?' he writes in a letter. [4] Rilke's point is that death itself should not be a part of life that won't go away, that cannot be transcended. Therefore, embrace it, but don't ignore it. Writers such as André Gide and Rilke keep coming back to this point because it is so important. The philosophical stance is not one of resignation to death, in a hopeless, pathetic, Christian sense, but in the acceptance of Taoism and Buddhism, which is really, deeply joyous, life-affirming, even radiant.

The emphasis on the void in Rilkean metaphysics has affinities with the philosophy of Taoism and Buddhism. Chuang-tzu, the very wonderful philosopher of ancient China, said, 'leap into the boundless and make it your home'. [5] This is precisely what Rilke's poems do: they indicate an infinite space of darkness and try to jump into it. The void is all absence but flips over to become all presence. This spiritual overturn is found in Christian mysticism. In the work of Meister Eckhart, a mystic, like Rilke, of the *via negativa*, the Godhead is described in terms of nothingness and darkness.

Mediæval mysticism is full of evocations of darkness – in Jan van Ruysbroeck, in *The Cloud of Unknowing*, and in Richard Rolle. Meister Eckhart spoke of descending down 'from nothingness to nothingness': the artist is always doing this (Samuel Beckett spoke of sitting at his work table for hours, sinking down into the darkness). In poets and mystics such as Dionysius the Areopagite, St John of the Cross, and Henry Vaughan, we hear of a radiant darkness, a 'superdazzling darkness'. The night is rich in mysticism, as it is in Rilke's poetry. So many of Rilke's poems exalt the night – not just in the *Poems To Night*, which echo Novalis' *Hymns To the Night*, but in so many other pieces.

In the art of Rainer Maria Rilke, we read passages such as this: 'I am open to clear Night's inflowing' (P/ 26, 164); 'Look up. How clear the night-space is tonight!' (ib., 267); the Night is also erotic, for in it desires have no visible limits – it is thus in many lyrics, and in many other poets' lyrics, a space where lovers and angels walk, rapt (ib., 110).

The poetic night has a powerful feminine flavour in Rainer Maria Rilke's work, as it does in so much of philosophy and poesie. In Taoism, the night corresponds to the *yin* essence, to female creativity and magic; in Indian mythology, black night is *Kali-yuga*, the time of chaos before regeneration, [6] while in the West, black signifies the occult, the hidden depths of the sixth sense, the præternatural faculties; in alchemy, a magical process which has many affinities with poetry, and with Rilke's poetry, the black stage is a part of the making of a magickal child, the *filius philosophorum*, created out of the conjoined King and Queen, the Sun and Moon of occultism; for poets, blackness is mysterious and prophetic – it speaks of secret wisdom, witchcraft, blood mysteries, growth and the unknown. In the black spaces, seeds grow: it is the space before time, the timeless place before time and mortality rush in to claim the individual and the body. For some poets, black is also Mother Night, the Great Goddess, the Mother of All, the cosmos itself, the feminine zone of metamorphosis and renewal. In the blackness, all things are regenerated. Night becomes womb.

All of these concepts and feelings merge together in the poetic mind, so that the poet can intuitively make connections between womb = growth = seeds = life = blossoming = love = magic = art/poetry = life = death = black = womb. The notions are not the same, they are equivalences, and they change continually. The poet's world is in flux, and Rilke's poetry proclaims change as a basis of life, in the Heraclitean manner.

All of these intuitive, poetic associations, of night and Mother Night, of blackness and occultism, of the night-space as the space/time of the cosmos or Great Mother, of the erotic, feminine nature of the night – are found in Rainer Maria Rilke's poetry, and in most major poets. The poet thus becomes a seed or self within the womb of the Earth, the space of the world. And what the poet records is the difference between the night spaces of secret magic which nourish her/ his soul, and the everyday, workaday world which suppresses magic and poetry. The poet's work (the poems) thus becomes a way of connecting day and night, ordinary life and secret, wild, magical, poetic life. The poem creates a bridge between the secret, twilit, inner world and the public, bright, outer world. Reading a poem enables one to get back to the secret, inner world, and the poet reminds us how important and nourishing the secret, inner world is.

The yearning of Rainer Maria Rilke for spaciousness, for the night, is both a desire for the comfort of the womb and a need for a gentle kind of obliteration. In total blackness, anything is possible, because there are no limits or laws. Partly because there are no people. Rilke's yearning for spacious blackness stems in part from his ambiguous attitudes towards people, his desire for contact, and his need for escape, his movements towards and away from relationships. The night-space is a place where he can be alone luxuriously. Rilke often spoke of being alone, of the need for solitude. With Rilke, we are always coming back to the self, to the quest for a maximum sense of selfhood. This may stem partly from the influence of Friedrich Nietzsche, who wrote in *The Anti-Christ*:

> The 'kingdom of God' is not something one waits for. It has no yesterday or tomorrow, it does not come 'in a thousand years' – it is an experience within a heart; it is everywhere, it is nowhere. [7]

Friedrich Nietzsche's precept is a familiar one now – that heaven or eternity or paradise is right inside us, and *now*. Joseph Campbell coined the phrase 'bliss is now' to cover this kind of mysticism. Taoism speaks of the 'eternal Now', the 'timeless moment', which is a key experience in most kinds of mysticism. The ecstasy is always there, for us to experience. One doesn't have to leap in agonized rapture, the *Tao Te Ching* says: you can have mystical ecstasy from a very quiet and peaceful experience:

> Limpid and still,
> One can be a leader in the empire. (106)

While other poets have a 'landscape of the soul', a space that is their own creation and refers to some part of the planet – a town, a house, a pastoral scene, a seascape – Rainer Maria Rilke's soul-space is abstract. Poets such as Francesco Petrarch have idealized landscapes that are manifestations of interior needs; Rilke's landscapes hardly touch so-called 'reality': instead, his poems operate in a dark, spacious soul-place that accords with the abstract, spiritual spaces of Islamic art, or the spatial mysteries of painters such as Piero della Francesca. Rilke enjoyed painting, and one can see how his poetic space corresponds with that of Early Renaissance art, with mediæval mysticism (in the illuminated *Book of Hours*), with the timeless, flat friezes of Ancient Egyptian and Ancient Greek art, and with the quiet intensity of Dutch still-life painting.

Rainer Maria Rilke's sense of poetic space is wholly internalized; that is, it works from an acute sense of the vast spaces inside oneself. It is essential, Rilke said, to use the 'generous spaces' inside us ('Seventh Elegy'). Rilke's sense of poetic space goes beyond the metaphysics of Symbolist art and becomes the symbol itself (see sonnet I.11 of *Sonnets To Orpheus*). In poems such as 'Archaic Torso of Apollo', we see the post-Symbolist sense of space emerging. It stems largely from Rilke's Auguste Rodin period, and his encounter with sculpture, when he was friends with the French sculptor (and wrote a study of his art). The sculpted work, like the dancer, actualizes space in a very powerful fashion. Inside becomes all outside. The dancer wildly becomes the space s/he moves within; the sculpture, too, sets

RILKE

alight the surrounding space (and the statue in 'Archaic Torso of Apollo' is in the process of coming alive, of being born).

In a lyric of 1924, Rilke says:

> Space spread transposingly from us to things:
> really to feel the way a tree upsrings,
> cast round it space from that which inwardly
> expands in you. (P/ 26, 310)

By enfolding the space around the object, the poet/ initiate sets it free, allowing it and the person to become themselves a little more. Rainer Maria Rilke's sense of poetics strips away the associations that have grown up around the object, and allows the onlooker to use the thing afresh. Every object has its own beingness, and the poet's job is to realize that beingness in poetry. This concept has something in common with the I-Thou relation of Martin Buber, and the concept of the 'It' of Georg Groddeck, which manifests itself through things.

Is this poetic, spatial philosophy mystical? Yes. But it is also quite ordinary. It gives objects the beingness which sculptors know all objects possess. It works in poetry as an attempt to produce an impersonal work – that is, a non-ego-bound portrait or depiction of the object itself. It becomes an attempt at presentation rather than re-presentation (i.e., a non-mediated event, not a picture of a thing, but the thing itself). The problem is that all poetry is representation, art, mediation. In poems such as 'The Bowl of Roses', Rilke tries to present us with the bowl of roses as they actually are, without ornamentation, without glib rhetoric, without tricks, rather in the manner of Paul Cézanne in his still-life paintings:

> Living in silence, endless opening out,
> space being used, but without space being taken
> from that space which the things around diminish;
> absence of outline, like untinted groundwork

and mere Within; so much so strangely tender
and self-illumined – to the very verge:
where do we know anything like this?

[...] And then the movement in the roses, look:
gestures deflected through such tiny angles,
they'd all remain invisible unless
their rays ran streaming out into the cosmos.

[...] And are not all just that, just self-containing,
if self-containing means: to take the world
and wind and rain and patience of the spring-time
and guilt and restlessness and muffled fate
and sombreness of evening earth and even
the melting, fleeing, forming of the clouds
and the vague influence of distant stars,
and change it to a handful of Within?

It now lies heedless in those open roses. (NP, 156-9)

Rainer Maria Rilke gives the impression of sitting before a bowl of roses in silence and trying to see the whole thing objectively, coolly, with the eye of a painter or a sculptor. Seeing the thing is one aspect, the 'in-seeing' which is explored in the next chapter: the opposite thrust is outwards, to expand the Within. This is the task of the poet when s/he is in her cosmic, transformative, shamanic mode. For Rilke, expansion is like breathing: the poet breathes out, like the god Orpheus with his singing, and fills the whole universe. The poet as an Orphic god sings things into existence, as an Australian aborigine mysticism.

This mystical expansion, by breath and voice and song, can work on a small scale, as in sonnet I.13 of *Sonnets To Orpheus,* where Rainer Maria Rilke talks of several fruits – banana, pear, apple:

What infinity!
Can't you feel inside your mouth a growing
mysteriousness, and where words were, a flowing

of suddenly released discovery? (SO/L, 59)

This fruitful expansion in the mouth activates several planes, including the erotic, the poetic, the linguistic, the synæsthetic (from taste to speech and beyond), and the religious (infinity in your mouth). The religious revolution within the body is equivalent in Rilke's poetics, and in symbolism, to a revolution in the cosmos, for the micro-cosmic and the macro-cosmic feed off each other (as Hermetic philosophy puts it: 'as above, so below'). Thus, the revelation of infinity from eating fruit in that special, Rilkean, attentive way, produces transformation at the cosmic level. Thus, in Rilkean metaphysics, where 'song is existence', breathing/ singing creates/ isolates/ activates the dark spaces (in sonnet II.1 of *Sonnets To Orpheus*).

The quest for inner realization in Rainer Maria Rilke's poetic is mirrored by a search for a soul-space, a 'bliss space', as Joseph Campbell called it, which is a combination of inside and outside, of thought and landscape. So in a letter to Princess Marie von Thurn und Taxis, Rilke wrote:

> But what I am most homesick for is the 'right place' – the *Elegy* place, which I am still hoping for and expecting: quiet, security for my real needs, nature, solitude, no people *at all* for six months! (LTT, 182)

Finding the place in reality was much more problematical than finding it in poetry, but poetry too is difficult. To be authentic means staying true to the structures and the strictures that are part of the medium, and partly self-imposed. In the *Duino Elegies*, the poet yearns for a space that is more psychic than actual – and it ignores society, families, relatives, labour, history, economics, politics, so many of the issues that people have to deal with in the real world:

> If only we too could discover a pure, contained, human place, our own

RILKE

strip of fruit-bearing soil between river and rock. (Mit, 161)

Finding that soul-space where one can flourish away from the eyes of an intolerant society is a dream of many lovers and poets. One recalled Sue and Jude Fawley, the ill-fated lovers in *Jude the Obscure* by Thomas Hardy. Much of art is born from the lack, the difference between the private fantasy and the public reality. For the dreamed-of bliss space exists everywhere and nowhere: it is now or never. The important thing is not that it is a fantasy and that poets and lovers are wasting their time dreaming their lives away; no, the key thing is the desire, the yearning, the burning. It is this desire that feeds so much of the artworks of the West: *Hamlet, The Divine Comedy, Wuthering Heights, Illuminations, Faust,* etc.

The big, breezy space of the poetry of Rainer Maria Rilke go straight to the emotional core of the reader. One is reminded of that poignant moment in D.H. Lawrence's novel *The Rainbow* when Tom Brangwen comes away from courting Lydia at her house and walks through the moonlit night: it is March and the wind tears holes in the clouds, and Tom feels as if his head is suddenly full of a dark, windy space. Here, in Rilke's poesie, the experience of being out at night mirrors exactly the interior state, so that one cannot distinguish between the two.

A poet such as Robert Graves, when walking at night would look for the moon, because he is a Goddess-dominated poet, and the moon is the symbol prime of the Goddess. Not so for Rilke: the moon is curiously lacking in his poetry (whereas in Graves, and in D.H. Lawrence, it is found everywhere). Rilke looks for the stars. His nights are radiant with stars, like the nights of the poet Henry Vaughan ('I saw Eternity the other night/ Like a great *Ring* of pure and endless light', from the poem 'The World'). The lovers, the Angel and the poet flourish in the starry night. Typical among Rilke's starlit nights is this passage from the

RILKE

'Third Elegy':

> Hark, how the night grows fluted and hollowed. You stars,
> is it not from you that the lover's delight in the loved one's
> face arises? Does not his intimate insight
> into her pure face come from the purest star? (DE/L, 41)

The starry, breezy night dominates the *Duino Elegies*: no matter how delicious Summers, dawns and meadows are, nights are rated highest in Rainer Maria Rilke's poetic world. In the 'Seventh Elegy', Rilke achieves a lucid, magical pantheism, a hymn to the natural world so ecstatic yet so convincing – the kind that only Arthur Rimbaud could achieve so effortlessly:

> Nicht nur die Morgen alle des Sommers –, nicht nur
> wie sie sich wandeln in Tag und strahlen vor Anfang.
> Nicht nur die Tag, die zart sind um Blumen, und oben,
> um die gestalteten Bäume, stark und gewaltig.
> Nicht nur die Andacht dieser entfalteten Kräfte,
> nicht nur die Wege, nicht nur die Wiesen im Abend,
> nicht nur, nach spätem Gewitter, das atmende Klarsein,
> nicht nur der mahende Schlaf und ein Ahnen, abends...
> sondern die Nächte! Sondern die hohen, des Sommers,
> Nächte, sondern die Sterne, die Sterne der Erde.
> O einst tot sein und sie wissen unendlich,
> all die Sterne: denn wie, wie, wie sie vergessen!
> (Not just all summer dawns, not just their turning to day, that light
> before first light. Not only tender days which lie soft about flowers,
> with above them the trees, sculptured, mighty and stark. Not only the
> loving devotion revealed by those powers; not only the paths, not only
> meadows at twilight, not that breathing at dusk, not that brightness
> which follows the storm; not only, when sleep draws near of an
> evening, the foretaste of knowledge just dawning... but the nights, but
> the nights too, those lofty nights of summer; but the stars too, the stars
> of the earth. O to lie dead at last; know them endlessly; all the stars;
> how could they – how could those be forgotten! DE/C, 57-59)

Oswald Spengler spoke of Ancient Greek drama occurring at noontide; William Shakespeare's plays take place in midafternoon, while John Wolfgang von Goethe's *Faust* and later dramas are of twilight. Certainly dusk is the time of Romanticism – in Heinrich Heine's verse, in Caspar David Friedrich's melancholy paintings, and, later, in the poems of Paul Verlaine and Charles Baudelaire (which celebrate crepuscular days in Paris). But, like Samuel Beckett, Rainer Maria Rilke goes deep into the night, where his poetry charts 'the curvings of my longing through the cosmos!' (P/ 26, 132). The goal of the journey into the night is how to 'make use' of the 'generous spaces' inside oneself ('Seventh Elegy'). The master of the night is of course the Angel: many poems outside the *Duino Elegies* evoke the Angel's control of the night, such as this poem, 'To the Angel', where the Angel is

> Strong, still light upon the verge of Being,
> burning out into nocturnal space... (P/ 26, 138)

More than lovers, heroes, children or poets, Angels set alight the 'inner space of night' (*Nachtinnenraum*); Angels soar 'keenly and unceasingly' through 'distant space ('Angels', Lem, 138). Rilke's poetry is night poetry – poetry that seems to have been composed at night, that speaks to the night-experiences of people. Rilke's poesie is always opening out onto something vast, dark, invisible, but rich. The void becomes all womb, and, in the opening out, self-conscoiusness turns to death-consciousness, which in turns makes life richer. And, ultimately, beingness may be achieved, as Rilke explained in a letter:

> In that supreme "open" World, all *exist* – one cannot say "simultaneously", for it is precisely the discontinuation of time which determines their existence. The past plunges everywhere into a deep Being. [8]

It is this kind of statement that scares critics, for here Rainer

RILKE

Maria Rilke is being mystical. Critics are quick to deny that Rilke was a mystic. But, mystic or not, he still made mystical pronouncements. All he's doing, as he says in the poem 'Gong', is a 'reversal of spaces. Projection of innermost worlds into the Open' (Mit, 283).

THREE

ESSENCE

> When I attempt to visualize my task, it becomes clear to me that it is not people about whom I have to speak, but things. Things. When I say the word (do you hear?) there is a silence; the silence which surrounds things. All movement subsides and becomes contour. And out of past and future time something permanent is formed: space, the great calm of objects which knows no urge.
>
> Rainer Maria Rilke, *The Rodin-Book* (46)

The movement is basically from absence to presence, and from presence to essence. In Rainer Maria Rilke's spatial mysticism, the presence/absence of objects is crucial: the space surrounding an object, a calm silence, reveals its presence. Contemplating the presence leads to a revelation of the object's essence. Essence is the soul or spirit or inner reality of a thing: presence is how this inner soul is manifested.

The 'in-seeing' of Rainer Maria Rilke is akin to *samadassana* in Zen Buddhism, as a recent authority of Zen Buddhism, D.T. Suzuki, explains:

RILKE

> Seeing is experiencing, seeing things in their state of suchness [*tathata*] or is-ness, Buddha's whole philosophy comes from this "seeing", this experiencing. [1]

In Zen Buddhism, in-seeing is essential: through it one begins the Eightfold Path towards enlightenment. Rainer Maria Rilke speaks of realizing the innerness (*Innigkeit*) of things: it is a sort of 'creative empathy'. [2] The idea is similar to James Joyce's notion of the 'epiphany', where there is a revelation of the radiance of an artwork. It is similar, too, to the fundamentals of symbolism, and how symbols are used. Rilke employs a umber of symbols – the rose, the night, stars, the Angel, Orpheus, the dancer – these items are not only symbols but powers and presences. As symbols, they induce the radiance so important to art:

> Symbols still maintain contact with the deep sources of life; they express, we may say, the "lived" spiritual... Symbolism *adds* a new value to an object or to an action without however disturbing their own proper and immediate values. In applying itself to an object or to an action, symbolism renders it "open". Symbolic thought makes the immediate reality "shine", but without diminishing or devaluating it: in its perspective the Universe is not closed, no object is isolated in its own existentialiness; every thing holds together in a closed system of correspondences and assimilations.

In this passage from *Symbolism, the Sacred and the Arts*, Mircea Eliade [3] shows how symbols multivalently engage a number of levels, from the visual through the Existential/ ontological, to the religious. Symbols open out onto the cosmos, or what Rainer Maria Rilke called 'the Open'. Symbols point past themselves as well as attracting attention to themselves as objects. Symbols also reveal, as Eliade notes, the inter-connectedness of things, what poets call the 'theory of correspondences' (the 'forest of symbols' of Charles Baudelaire in *Flowers of Evil*). We have already noted that in Rilke's poesie we can move from womb to birth to love to death to timelessness, and so on. One symbol melts into another: from Rilke's rose (and all poets' roses – from Dante Alighieri through William Shakespeare to today's poets), we can move to images of the Goddess, vulvas, birth, Christianity, mysticism, and so on. Once the radiance of poetry has been activated, through the right use of the right symbol at the right time, we can travel anywhere. This openness is central to Rilke's poetics, and is central to the experience of poetry. For mediæval poets, symbolism leads to God – through the Mystic Rose and the angelic hierarchies of the Godhead. In 20th century poetry, symbolism leads to an experience of openness and space. This 'Open' is no less mystical than the God of mediæval Christianity. It doesn't have the same authority of the centuries that the Christian deity has, but it is no less authentic, meaningful, desired and needed. In the *Sonnette an Orpheus* (11.13), Rilke writes:

> Be – and yet know the great void where all things began,
> the infinite source of your inmost vibration,
> so that, this once, you may give it your perfect assent. (Mit, 245)

Rainer Maria Rilke's poetic in-seeing corresponds to Martin Heidegger's philosophy of being and presence, where being is manifested through presence. Rilke's Grail or goal of beingness is extremely difficult to achieve, and is fraught with Existential despair and doubt. In a Heideggerian mood, Rilke said of the transformation of the *Neue Gedichte*, 'it had to arrive at the essence'. [4] His notion of in-seeing and thereness comes partly from fine art, from the extended contemplation of sculpture (his time with Auguste Rodin). In a fragment of an 'Elegy', Rilke speaks of the 'infinite there of statues'. [5] Statues fascinate him: 'they *are*. That is all', he wrote to Lou Andreas-Salomé. [6] The aim is a new kind of objectivity, an emphasis on forms, a silent receptivity, a distanced but involved perception. In a letter of Feb

RILKE

17, 1914 to Magda, Rilke wrote:

> I love in-seeing. Can you imagine with me how glorious it is to in-see a dog, for example, as you pass it – by *in-see* I don't mean to look *through*... what I mean is to let yourself precisely into the dog's centre, the point from which it begins to be a dog.

And he continues to say that his

> earthly bliss was... again and again, here and there, in such in-seeing – in the indescribably swift, deep, timeless moments of this godlike in-seeing. [7]

This stance stems from the Western, hermetic tradition, from Neoplatonism and occult philosophy. Lawrence Durrell has a similar theory of the heraldic 'sigil', as he called it, the essence of a thing. The wonderful sculptor Constantin Brancusi spoke of wanting to get at the 'essence of things' in his art. Brancusi's sculptures were not abstract at all, he maintained, but supremely realist. His sculpted works are even more accomplished than those of Rilke's guru, Auguste Rodin. In pieces such as *Bird In Space, Fish, Head* and *Lovers,* Brancusi caught in stone the essence of his subjects. Brancusi's æsthetic 'interiorization' is similar to Rilke's: it is a means of realizing concretely the presence of a subject – in a poem for Rilke, in a sculpture for Brancusi. [8] Brancusi's sculptures, like all sculptures, create sacred space within profane space; similarly, Rilke's poems make sacred space out of chaos. A neopagan or Japanese Shintoist might build a shrine in their own home, or perhaps in a grove; earlier peoples constructed stone circles, temples, altars and such. In a corresponding fashion, the poet builds, piece by piece, line by line, word by word, a poem. The poem is very distinctly a sacred space within profane, everyday, public space. Like a garden, the poem is very conscious of its edges, where its sacrality ends and profane space begins.

RILKE

For Rainer Maria Rilke, the problem was not one of self-expression, as it was for Samuel Beckett, but of transcending the form of poetry to produce the thing-in-itself – not the experience of a feeling, but the feeling itself. Rilke's theory of 'Kunst-Ding', his notion of thingness, stems from his contemplation of the art of, among others, Paul Cézanne and Auguste Rodin. D.H. Lawrence's reading of Cézanne's work is similar: Lawrence talks of the brilliance of Cézanne's ability to present the viewer with the essence of object such as apples. Cézanne shows us the appleness of apples, Lawrence claimed. Finding and presenting the isness of things is the painter's aim: Rilke made it the poet's aim also. Of Rodin, Rilke wrote:

> Pose, group, composition, none of the these things any longer existed. Only an endless variety of living surfaces, only life... (R, 9)

In poems such as 'Archaic Torso of Apollo', Rainer Maria Rilke showed how to create a sense of 'living surfaces': the torso actually comes alive. In other poems, Rilke tries to paint objects in the manner of Paul Cézanne – some of the finest examples occur in 'The Panther', 'The Gazelle', 'The Bowl of Roses', 'Blue Hydrangea' and 'The Parks'. Critics usually cite the poems 'The Panther' and 'Archaic Torso of Apollo' as the best expressions of Rilke's thing-poems, and rightly. Here we will quote from 'Blue Hydrangea', which fully represents Rilke's propensity for Cézannean art:

> Like the last green in the palette's colour
> these leaves are rough and dry and dull in hue
> under the topmost blossoms where the blue
> touches the petals as from a far mirror.
>
> A mirror stained with tears, that is not clear,
> they wish to vanish from it: they are shadowy
> as blue letter paper of a long past year

RILKE

that is tinged with yellow, violet and grey... (Lem, 77)

Like a painter, Rainer Maria Rilke draws out the colour and tone of the flowers, while he moves towards a self-reflexive metaphysics in his use of echoing devices, such as, here, the mirror, or, in the other poems, references to eyes gazing, poets speaking, to windows, eyes and onlookers (manifestations of Rodinesque 'eye-work').

Love plays a part in this in-seeing: for the viewer, says Rainer Maria Rilke, throws a silence calm around the object. In other words, the essence of the object needs the viewer to make itself manifest. The gazer is an integral part of the metaphysics of essence through presencing. Only in art can essence truly fulfil itself, Rilke maintains. Long before Jacques Lacan, Rilke had spoken of the pleasure of looking ('Gazing is a wonderful thing' [10]). In Lacanian psychology, seeing is desire in action; the act of looking enhances the onlooker more than the object; the look is erotic, but the act of gazing is ultimately narcissistic; in elevating the object, the viewer elevates her/ himself. All of this is present in Rilke's theory of in-seeing, his contemplation of objects, in poems such as 'The Gazelle' and 'The Rose-Window'.

In Rilke's poetics, the methodology of in-seeing is erotic as well as metaphysical. What Rilke wants to do is to show us his desire for the object as well as the object itself. Thus, the poem 'The Panther' is an erotic poem not only because of its subject – the sensuality of the animal – but because of the erotic field of meaning the poet throws around the beast, which comes out so powerfully in the poem. Of 'mood painters', Rilke had written, 'they painted: I love this; instead of painting: there it is'. [11] Rilke too would like poems to say, 'I love this', rather than just, 'this is here'. Rilke loves many of his subjects – the sleek gazelle in the poem 'The Gazelle' is the 'enchanted one', and the poet is mesmerized by the animal (as Rilke said he was in real life, before the making of the poem). Rilke's symbols are all adored, in varying degrees of ambivalence: rose, mirror, dancer, sculpture, statue, tree, flower, Angel, Orpheus, etc.

What happens is that Rainer Maria Rilke's concept of in-seeing and innerness makes the poetic connection between the essence of the object and the essence of the poet. In other words, Rilke the poet identifies with the interior of the object. There are times when one sees the poet wishing if not to dissolve into the object (like the soul into God in traditional mysticism), then at least to partake of the same innerness the object possesses. Thus, the poet wants her/ his interior to be like the essence of a rose, for instance. Extending this argument further, we can say that when Rilke is describing the innerness of a rose, he is also describing his own interior. In Rilke's poetics, objects are mirrors, and when the subject of a poem is the soul of an object, it can be equivalent to (though not always the same as) the soul of the poet.

Rainer Maria Rilke's is a poetry of interiority in the tradition of much of love poetry, but without dwelling upon love as the vehicle of that interiority. While poets such as Dante Alighieri, William Shakespeare and Francesco Petrarch used love as a pretext, an excuse, for investigating the notion of selfhood, Rilke dwells upon being as a mean of questioning selfhood. While love poets prate of love, Rilke speaks of space and being. In his art, the thrust outwards, into the wild, dark spaces, mirror the descent down, like Orpheus, into the underworld of the self. Rilke knows, as Sigmund Freud did, that the inner spaces of humans far exceed in depth and strangeness the vast spaces of the universe out there. Rilke speaks of 'the *depth-dimension*, of our inner being, which does not even need the spaciousness of the universe to be, in itself, almost unlimited'. [12]

Rainer Maria Rilke's dimension is the vertical one that leads down – mythically, to the black underworld, psychologically, to the unconsciousness, to the foundations of the psyche, spiritually, to the seat of the soul, the Ground of Being, and poetically, into a wild, dark space. Mysticism speaks of 'vertical meditation', which is a going down to the depths of being. In mysticism, self-purgation is essential: most mysticisms stress the need to deny the ego, the self. Self-purification is the first stage in mystical process: the idea is that the less there is of the soul, the more there is of God. Rilke, like Samuel Beckett, is a poet who goes with the notion that 'less is more', but, like Beckett, like most poets, he does not let go of the ego. In most Western mysticism, there is always something left of the self in the soul-God union. Western mystics tend to hang on to that last part of themselves, whereas Oriental mystics are more severe and ascetic, and let it all go.

Like Ludwig Wittgenstein and Samuel Beckett, Rainer Maria Rilke stresses the limits of language – there is a space which lies beyond description in words. But that beyond-words place is within the self. It is a place where animals live naturally (the 'Open'); flowers blossom into that space. 'All Nature stirs inside with living essence', Rilke wrote in the *Late Poems* (BR, 141). It is a place, though, that can only be found in art, ultimately, except in a few cases where art spills over into mysticism and the artist lives as a mystic. We can see that Rilke is a mystic; that is, the Rilke-poet who comes out of the poems is mystical. But whether Rilke in real life was a mystic or not is not our concern here. Biographers tend to deny the mystical connection. In Rilke's works, however, there is no doubt – as in this superb line from the *Duino Elegies*:

> Nirgends, Geliebte, wird Weit sein, als innen. Unser
> Leben geht hin mit Verwandlung.
> (Nowhere, beloved, can world exist but within.
> Life passes in transformation. [DE/L, 70-71])

Of course world must be within; it is that first, before everything follows. A few lines earlier the poet writes, 'Hiersein ist herrlich', translated by J.B. Leishman as, 'life here's glorious!'

RILKE

(DE/L, 71); by S. Cohn as, 'being is marvellous!' (DE/C, 59); and by Stephen Mitchell as, 'truly being here is glorious' (Mit, 189).

Of course being here is glorious. This is not ecstasy but a simple affirmation of life. Being here is also horrible, difficult mad, painful, strange; but it is marvellous, too. The artist's job, like the mystic's job, is to realize this glorious sense of beingness. As Rilke put it in his *Letters On Cézanne*: 'all we basically have to do is to *be*, but simply, earnestly, the way the earth simply is' (Cez, 69). This is mystical statement, but it is also completely ordinary. Of course we have 'to *be*', like the Earth simply '*is*', because we are part of the Earth. What Rilke means, and so many poets mean, is that we have to stop the fretful striving to be anything other than ourselves. The goal of simple beingness, simple thereness, is actually difficult to attain. Rilke can't (or won't) tell us how. Very few poets or mystics do tell us how. Poets do not preach or teach in that pedagogical manner. They hint, suggest, point, but always in ambiguous, opaque, obscure ways, even when they are at their clearest. D.H. Lawrence also wailed, 'why can't we simply *be*, as the horse or the sunflower simply *is*'; but Lorenzo was in his life very unsatisfied – always travelling about restlessly, just like Rilke.

For Rainer Maria Rilke, the Angel was the apotheosis of beingness in life, and unattainable. The Angel was too severe: Orpheus embodied a different kind of beingness, no less rich, but gentler, brighter. If Rilke couldn't achieve the beingness of the Angel in life, he could at least attain the beingness of Orpheus in poetry. Attaining maximum selfhood is a prime objective in Rilkean metaphysics. There are correspondences here with Oriental mysticism, with the *tat tvam asi* of Hindu religion ('Thou Art That'), [13] where the quest is for the mystical realization that self and Self (Brahma) are one. This mystical oneness is notoriously difficult to achieve. In the West, C.G. Jung termed the Buddhist quest for self-realization 'individuation', which is, he said, the 'process by which a person becomes a psychological 'individual', that is, a separate, indivisible unity or 'whole'.' [14] Clearly, this is the quest of Malte in Rilke's troubled novel. The urge towards individuation is not simply the 'coming of the ego into consciousness', writes Jung, but an urge towards wholeness. [15]

The struggle of many an Existential outsider is for being and wholeness (André Gide's Michel, Albert Camus' Mersault, J.-K. Huysmans' Des Esseintes, Jean-Paul Sartre's Rosquentin and John Cowper Powys's Wolf Solent). Malte in Rilke's novel does not achieve it, and, much later, in the *Sonnets To Orpheus* the poet is still crying out, 'But when can *we* be real?' (Mit, 231). The god of poetry, Orpheus, achieves beingness easily, it seems to the still-becoming poet. What the poet has to do is to concentrate on her/his withinness. This alone is real, and rich, and will enable beingness to blossom. 'Only within is near; all else is far', noted Rilke in 'The Island' (NP, 139), meaning the self must be the best realm for developing a sense of beingness, for moving from becoming to beingness.

Ripening or blossoming is a major theme for Rainer Maria Rilke, most especially in the *Sonnets To Orpheus,* but the urge towards beingness is a main element in poems such as 'Archaic Torso of Apollo', 'Turning-Point', 'What birds plunge through' and 'Requiem For a Friend'. The realm of blossoming is what Rilke calls the 'heart-space' (*Herzraum*): 'The deepest space *in* us' (Mit, 147). An important step for Rilke is to move into the 'heart-space' and make it one's home, much as the Chinese philosopher Chuang-tzu said of the void: one must get into 'right attention', as Buddhist say, with the 'heart-space', much as the initiate in the 'Third Elegy' of the *Duino Elegies* does:

> Loved. Doted on all that wildness
> inside him. Loved and gave himself up to exploring
> the primitive beckoning forest within him... (DE/C, 35)

RILKE

It is inside the alienated self of the bourgeois poet that the Baudelairean forest of symbols can flourish. The means that Rainer Maria Rilke employs derives from the materiality of language developed by Stéphane Mallarmé and Paul Valéry. Rilke's mysticism of language extends forward to the Minimal art of the 1960s, where artists such as Tony Smith talked about being interested only in the art object itself, not in effects, which come afterwards and are the responsibility of the viewer or consumer. In the art of Frank Stella, Jasper Johns and Barnett Newman, there is a passionate concern with the art object as a Sartrean thing-in-itself, resplendent in its own beingness, its own material presence. The frame of the painting, the support, the way the canvas is pinned to the stretcher, the distance of the painting from the wall, all these things become important in 1960s art. The inside became all outside. Construction was deemed crucial. In a similar way, Rilke's post-Symbolist, modernist poems call attention to themselves as artistic constructs.

While stressing the materiality of the word, Symbolist poets and those who succeeded them (Rilke, Stein, Beckett), also admit the inadequacy of language to get at those transcendent realms which have increasingly become the province of poetry since the Renaissance. The 'literature of the unword' is the term Samuel Beckett gives for a poetry founded on ambiguity and difficulty: Rilke is more optimistic. He holds that poetry can suggest the vast space by concentrating on absence: the poet as Orpheus can fill the vast void with her/ his breathing: space becomes music and song = existence.

FOUR

ANGELS

> The "Angel" of the *Elegies* has nothing to do with the angel of the Christian heaven... The Angel of the *Elegies* is the creature in whom that transformation of the visible into the invisible we are performing already appears completed.
>
> Rainer Maria Rilke, letter [1]

The function of Rainer Maria Rilke's Angel is to provide a model for the transformation the poet is trying to accomplish: that of attaining fullness of being, of achieving self-transcendence, of moving out (in) to the wide, black spaces. The Angel is the embodiment of a fully achieved life potential, the manifestation of the invisible. The Angel is fully alive, has achieved transcendence. The Angel is something of a magician, a shaman (the shaman is the ancestor of the angelic figure), and, not least, something of a Nietzschean *Übermensch*, as Walter Kauffmann notes in *From Shakespeare To Existentialism*. [2]

The Rilkean Angel is not a fixed, unchanging entity, but something in a state of delicious and delirious flux. [3] The Angel is the supreme warrior and Grail Knight, a præternatural traveller between the earthly and the otherworldly realms (like the shaman). The Angel is a being in whom transcendence is gloriously achieved. Rilke's spiritual goal is transcendence into being. This is depicted in his poetry as a magical flight into dark space. The master of magical flight is the archaic shaman, and the angel. The image of 'he who understands has wings' – as the *Pancavimca Brahmana* says: 'he who understands has wings'. [4] All things wish to fly, says Rilke, in the fourteenth sonnet of Part Two of *Sonnets To Orpheus*:

> All things want to fly. Only *we* are weighed down by desire,
> caught in ourselves and enthralled with our heaviness.
> Oh what consuming, negative teachers we are
> for them, while eternal childhood fills them with grace. (Mit, 247)

The Angel in the *Duino Elegies* is the poet's Virgil who guides him towards the Mystic Rose of pure beingness. Becoming an Angel is a terrifying transformation but also a beautiful one: beauty and terror are mixed in equal measure in the Angel.

The Angel is terrifying too because we humans are 'not-angels', as Keith May says in *Nietzsche and Modern Literature*. [5] The Angel is at once everything we are not, and everything we should be. The problem with the Angel, though, is that it doesn't live here, on Earth, but either in Heaven or in Hell, either in the land of the more-than-alive or the more-than-dead. The Angel moves closer to us to show us what we might become: in the 'Second Elegy', the Rilke-poet invokes the Angel, who arrives, and displays it powers:

> Fortune's favourites, early-successful,
> destiny-pampered; you stand as our very peaks
> and our summit, seem crested and touched
> by the rose of Creation; pollen of Godhead's own flowering;
> limbs of light; paths, stairways, thrones,

realms of pure being; emblazoned delight;
riots of sense's enchantments: and, of a sudden, alone –
you are mirrors: you pour out your beauty
but your faces gather it back to yourselves. (DE/C, 26-27)

Rainer Maria Rilke says that his Angel is not that of Christianity, but it displays many of the qualities of the archangels of the *Old Testament*, and of the Archangel Gabriel as occult messenger, and of St Michael as holy warrior; also, Rilke invokes in that famous first line of the *Duino Elegies* the hierarchies of angels:

Who, if I cried, would hear me among the angelic
orders? (DE/L, 25)

which come straight from the writings of Dionysius the Areopagite, whose wonderfully vivid depictions in Neo-platonic terms of the celestial realms so inspired Dante Alighieri in the *Divina Commedia*.

Other ancestors of Rilke's Angel include the angels of Jewish and Qabbalic magic; the occult angels of William Blake and John Dee; and the *divas* of Hinduism. Angels, at once erotic, spiritual, awesome, strange, multi-sexual, prophetic, apocalyptic, child-like and utterly other, appear in the works of many poets: in Dante Alighieri's art and the Italian *stilnovisti*, in the work of William Shakespeare, Henry Vaughan ('How like an angel came I down!'), Thomas Traherne, Arthur Rimbaud, etc. An angel is a being who excites many poets, as they mesmerize many painters (and filmmakers).

In the famous letter to his Polish translator, Witold von Hulewicz, of Nov 13, 1925, Rainer Maria Rilke explains the function of the Angel: to show us, humans, how to be painfully and blissfully alive. In the figure of the Angel, the transcendence into the Open, that realm of pure being, is complete. Rilke writes:

RILKE

> Transformed? Yes, for our task is to stamp this provisional, perishing earth into ourselves so deeply, so painfully and passionately, that its being may rise again, "invisibly", in us. (DE/L, 157)

This philosophical stance is familiar to us now from the writing of Albert Camus, Jean-Paul Sartre, Martin Heidegger, Friedrich Nietzsche, André Gide and Henry Miller. This view argues for a life founded on accentuated perception, a life where all the senses are cleansed so that experience can be extraordinary. Rilke describes the realm of the Angels, that realm of 'pure being', in the 'Seventh Elegy' (quoted above, page 54). In the letters, he circumscribes that zone:

> there is neither a here nor a beyond, but only the great unity, in which the "Angels", those beings that surpass us, are at home. (Cez)

This 'great unity', where Angels live, is a place Rainer Maria Rilke would love to be, but he is reconciled to the impossibility of ever getting there. In his earlier poetry, before the *Duino Elegies*, he stresses the other-worldliness of the Angel. Angels appear in the *Book of Pictures, New Poems, Uncollected Poems* and the *Sonnets To Orpheus*. In poems such as 'Annunciation', the visitation of the Archangel Gabriel is described in Rilke's spatial mysticism. The spatial emphasis occurs also in the poems 'To the Angel', 'L'Ange du Meridien', 'The Angel' and 'Angels'. The Angels of the early poems – the guardian angels and creatures of light – stem from the angels of Early Renaissance art as much as from occultism or religion: but in poems such as 'Requiem', Rilke indicates that he was forming a sophisticated ideology of the Angel before writing the *Duino Elegies*, and which could perform special rites in the realm of beingness:

> I want to form an angel from that sense
> and hurl him upward, into the front rank

of screaming angels, reminding God. (Mit, 83)

One can't do better than an Angel, Rainer Maria Rilke claims. The Angel is refined way beyond humans. Lovers are close to the Angel's state of being, but, says Rilke in the *Elegies*, their partner, the beloved, gets in the way of the lovers achieving beingness (Mit, 193). The Angels work within a religious hierarchy which humans must adhere to if they are going to follow the correct mystical processes to attain angelhood. One must be at least a poet; and beyond that, a lover; and beyond that, a more-tha-human: transcendence through a hierarchy of ontological states (states of being). The requirements, practically, are stillness, silence, solitude, meditation and rigorous commitment.

The condition of the Rilkean Angel is ruthlessly ascetic: it goes beyond love, poetry, art, music, politics, language, time, society, the family and religion. To reach the Angels' realm one must be patient, as the fruit is on the tree, in the poem 'The Fruit':

And through a whole long summer fructified
within that day and night travailing tree
and felt itself as urging instancy
to meet responding space outside. (SW, 340)

Once the angelic state is achieved, there is celestial joy, and a devouring sense of mystery and infinity. When the tree of poetry bears fruit the results can be extraordinary, as the thirteenth sonnet of Part One of *Sonnets To Orpheus* says: 'to experience, feeling, joy – celestial!' (SO/L, 59). At this stage, words such as *death, infinity, being* and *mystery* lose their meaning and blur into one. Their musicality is their only attribute that remains. As Rilke says, 'Affirmation of life-AND-death turns out to be one in the *Elegies*'. [7] Duality is destroyed, which is one of the hallmarks of the sacred when it is renewed. Rilke demonstrates the '*identity* is dreadfulness and bliss', [8] which is a mythic state, a primæval state of unity. It is a state of vertical meditation, a silent, still condition of deep contemplation, out and in the world, the endpoint of the *via negativa*, the negative way of Christian and Buddhist mysticism. In the *Duino Elegies*, it is described in the terms of Oriental philosophy, in terms of 'not-this-not-that':

> We never find that nowhere, free from
> negatives, unsupervised and pure; the place
> which we might breathe and know unendingly,
> and never crave. While we stay children, we
> can get lost in that stillness – till something
> jogs us from it. Or someone dies and *is* it. (DE/C, 65)

Poem after poem celebrates this spaceless space where deities such as Buddha, Hermes, Apollo, Venus and the Goddess live. Music helps the initiate on her/ his ontological journey to the vast realm of pure being: music is ever a preoccupation of Rainer Maria Rilke, Paul Verlaine and Stéphane Mallarmé – embodied in the musicality of their poetries. Angels, of course, have long been musical – they play trumpets, drums, harps and sing in heavenly choirs. Music is a way of activating the dark, poetic space for Rilke: it helps to create the spiritual bridge between here and there, between human life and that of the Angels.

Talk of being, dark spaces and the Angels brings us to a major theme in Rainer Maria Rilke's art: solitude. One imagines the Rilkean poet to be absolutely alone somewhere, an isolation similar to that of another restless, Middle European thinker, Ludwig Wittgenstein, who used to retire hermit-like to a hut beside a lake that one could only reach by boat. The Rilkean poet must be similarly acquainted with silence and solitude. No people, no love, no touch, no conversation, no contact. Just the inner self, quietly flowering all by itself, nurtured by an insomnia and a letter out of the blue, every two months or so.

RILKE

This background of stillness and solitude forms the stuff of many a poem by Rainer Maria Rilke, such as the sonnet "What still around a soul!": the sestet reads thus:

> this stillness around a god, but will this compare?
> Wait! Is it not growing stiller and stiller, progressing
> in stillness, until you can feel it pressing
>
> your throbbing heart, whose beat has beaten a way
> into some soundless pause in the day?...
> He is there. (SW, 331)

Like a monk or ascetic – of Taoism, Buddhism, or Catholicism – Rainer Maria Rilke the poet always emphasizes the need for solitude. Through silence one attains stillness; stillness is essential for realization, say Taoist philosophers such as Chuang-tzu and Lao-tzu. ('If only stillness reigned, pure, elemental', says the narrator of the seventh poem in the *Book of Hours* (SW, II, 30)). Solitude is easier to attain in art than in life, and Rilke's problem was to make life like his poetry. In many letters, he wrote of his need for isolation (this one was to Nanny Wunderly):

> *Solitude* is the *only* possible thing for me. [9] What's need is just this loneliness, vast inner loneliness. [10] Never forget that solitude is my lot, that I must not have a need for anyone. [11] It is good to be solitary, for solitude is difficult. (LYP, 31). [Solitude] is fundamentally not something we can choose or reject. We *are* solitary. (ib., 37)

The problem is that though Rainer Maria Rilke the poet might love solitude, Rilke the man clearly craves company. It is an ambivalence that many have wrestled with, but not resolved satisfactorily. To be utterly alone is to be inhuman or non-human, as Weston La Barre notes: it is impossible to be completely alone, anyway, because every individual is wholly enculturated – filled to the brim with culture, with other people's thoughts, ideas, feelings, etc. You can't escape people because they are inside you.

RILKE

Every person may be an island, but they live on islands populated, like Prospero's island in *The Tempest*, with many spirits and beings. Ultimately, the urge towards total solitude produces the outsider effect of Malte in Rilke's novel:

> It is ridiculous. Here I sit in my little room, I, Brigge, who have to be twenty-eight years old and of whom no one knows. I sit here and am nothing. And nevertheless this nothing begins to think and think, five flights up, on a grey Parisian afternoon, these thoughts: Is it possible, it thinks, that one has not yet seen, known and said anything real or important? …Yes, it is possible. (28)

FIVE

GODDESS

The transforming experience which then seized me at a hundred places at once, emanated from the great reality of your being. I had never before, in my groping hesitancy, felt life so much, believed in the present, and recognized the future so much. You were the opposite of all doubt and witness to the fact that everything you touch, reach and see exists.

Rainer Maria Rilke, letter to Lou Andreas-Salomé (November, 1903
[1]

There are many biographies published about Rainer Maria Rilke, so we will not investigate Rilke's life in detail. But there is one aspect of Rilke's life that seems to shed light on his poetry: his relationship with Lou Andreas-Salomé (mainly during the years 1897-1901). Andreas-Salomé (1861-1937) was an extraordinary person who was romantically associated with Friedrich Nietzsche, and was later a pupil of Sigmund Freud; she knew Hans Hofmannsthal, Arthur Schnitzler, Jakob Wassermann, Richard Wagner, Count Eduard Keyserling, Joseph Conrad, Franz

RILKE

Wedekind, Leo Tolstoy, Ivan Turgenev and Georg Brandes. 'Europe's cultural élite paid hommage to Lou Salomé', remarked H.F. Peters. [2] Nietzsche was besotted with her for a while. He called her

> sharp-sighted as an eagle and courageous as a lion and yet, in spite of it all, a very child-like girl. [3]

Child-like she might have been to Friedrich Nietzsche, but Lou Andreas-Salomé was in fact a formidable presence, intellectually and socially. Her effect on Rilke was massive, and bound up with his experiences of Russia, with his child-like notions of motherhood, with his love of the Madonnas in Italian Renaissance paintings, and with his artistic hunger. For Andreas-Salomé, her affair with Rilke was at times joyous, when, she said, 'body and soul [were] indivisible one'. [4]

Rainer Maria Rilke fell passionately in love with Lou Andreas-Salomé, as the letters testify. The extract quoted above is typical: other sections reveal just how deep, and long-lasting, his affection for her was:

> You were the right door through which I entered into the open. [5];
> You can explain to me what I do not understand, you can tell me what I should do; you know what I must, and what I need not fear [6] I am in you! [7]

Lou Andreas-Salomé's effect on Rainer Maria Rilke was to refine his ideas and opinions way beyond the level they had reached. Her notions of love as a supra-sexual sacrament, a 'kneeling together', we find emerging later on, after the affair was over, in Rilke's poetry. Andreas-Salomé's intellectual powers astonished Rilke – 'She moves fearlessly midst the most burning mystery', he said of her. [8] As Wolf Lappmann remarked,

> This love, transformed through the years into a deep friendship, was

RILKE

an unexpected boon that would live on as a permanent feature of Rilke's inner landscape. [9]

In his letters to Lou Andreas-Salomé, Rainer Maria Rilke is at his most rapturous, within an erotic context. Later, in his poetry, after the years of his romance with Andreas-Salomé (from 1897 to 1901), the erotic charge moves from human to angelic emotions, from earthly to otherworldly love.

Lou Andreas-Salomé called Rainer Maria Rilke a typical psycho-neurotic in her psychoanalytical notes: she gradually extricated herself from being romantically involved with Rilke, although they remained friends until his death. [10] One of her Andreas-Salomé's important legacies was to tell Rilke to work and work; this was also Auguste Rodin's battle cry: *'il faut travailler*, one must go on working.' In his *New Poems*, Rilke worked at length to produce the kind of poem he knew was possible, in that Rodinesque, craftsman-like way.

While Lou Andreas-Salomé distanced herself from Rainer Maria Rilke, he did the same. She later wrote: 'For all the caring fervour of our relationship, I stood detached'. [11] For a time, at least, though, Andreas-Salomé was clearly a Muse for Rilke, a supremely powerful woman who embodied the feminine principle at its most potent. Rilke's attitudes to women and to sexuality were always ambivalent. He had many female friends, and many of his collections of letters are to women. Obviously, women were very important for him, but he remained confused about them. His view of his own sexual identity was ambiguous – he disliked his body, for instance, and the way it intruded upon his thoughts: he wanted to live in a spiritual realm, he wrote to Andreas-Salomé, but moans, 'why must I be informed of every noise in my body, which annoys and distracts me and involves me in the mystery of the smallest things?' [12] This is a typical masculinist view: my body 'informs me' of noises. Rilke is psychically detached from his body, in the same way that the early Christian theologians from St Paul through Tertullian, Origen and St Augustine to Thomas Aquinas and beyond have stressed the split between soul and body, spirit and flesh. In Christianity, the body's evil, sinful, mere base matter. Such disturbing views, so hopelessly wrong and neurotic, became the foundation of Western religion. Rilke is part of this body-hating, which extends in Christian thought to woman-hating. It manifests itself in Rilke's poetry as a yearning for bodily transcendence, a desire for escape into pure space and being.

Feminine magic and the figure of the Goddess does play an important role in Rainer Maria Rilke's poetics. Rilke is not a Goddess worshipper, like, says, John Keats or Dante Alighieri. Rilke did not compose a cycle of love poems, like Francesco Petrarch or John Donne. Rilke's Goddess is no personage, no Dark Lady, or Muse-woman, no particular person, but more a feeling, an atmosphere (although he did compose many poems for particular women). Rilke is very excited by the female artist, for instance – a sculptor or dancer. One of his finest poems, the 'Requiem For a Friend', centres around a female artist, while the dancer Vera Knoop dances at the centre of the *Sonnets To Orpheus*. Poems such as 'Annunciation', 'Prayer To the Virgin', 'Cretan Artemis', 'Eve', 'Maidens', 'Leda', 'Nike' and 'Endymion' are clearly Goddess-oriented lyrics, or poems infused with a powerful sense of the feminine. But others, such as the rose poems, are also soaked in Goddess imagery. In his *Life of Mary* cycle, which mirrors the mediæval *Book of Hours*, Rilke modulates and comments on each stage in the Virgin's life story. More convincing, perhaps, given Rilke's anti-Christianity, are the poems dedicated to, about or alluding to pre-Christian Goddesses, such as Leda, Artemis, Venus and Eurydice. These deities are distinctly eroticized – in 'Leda' in particular, but also in 'Birth of Venus', where the Rilke-poet focusses on the body of the Goddess,

RILKE

on her breasts, thighs, belly, loins and vagina, which is

> like a group of silver birch in April,
> warm, empty, all unhidden. (NP, 153)

The most famous depiction of the Goddess occurs in 'Orpheus. Eurydice. Hermes', which centres on the mystery and solitude of the Goddess:

> She was deep within herself, like a woman heavy
> with child, and did not see the man in front,
> nor of the road ascending into life,
> withdrawn within herself; filled to the brim
> with that great fullness of her having died.
> Full as a fruit with sweetness and with darkness
> her great death filled her; and it was so new,
> that comprehension failed her utterly.
>
> She had come into a new virginity
> and was untouchable; her sex was closed
> like a young flower at nightfall;
> her hands, so unused to marriage rites,
> felt the light god's gentle and guiding touch
> repellent, as too intimate and close. (Mit, 51-53; Butler, 202)

Rainer Maria Rilke's eroticism in his poetry is marked by delicacy and ambiguity. The Goddess, as here, is in ascension. She travels far beyond the man, her consort. Her transformation is deeper than his. Rilke is a deeply feminized poet, one acutely attuned to the feminine inside him:

> Learn, inner man, to look on your inner woman,
> the one attained from a thousand
> natures, the merely attained but
> not yet beloved form. (Mit, 135)

In Rainer Maria Rilke's poetics, to use Carl Jung's terms, the *anima* is not projected outwards, as in the poetry of Francesca

RILKE

Petrarch, who created Laura de Sade, the mirror of his own unconscious desires; rather, in Rilke's poetics the *anima* is interiorized, but at a level so deep and dark, it is impossible to talk about it. Even poetry has problem engaging it; there is always a final ambiguity in Rilke's poetics, and in his words, which no amount of clarification can dispel. The 'heart-work', indicated in the above poem, 'Turning-Point', is Rilke's form of Freudian dream-work. 'Heart-work' for Rilke is the process of giving birth to oneself through the mechanisms of art. The artist rebirths her/ himself every time s/he creates an artwork. The process is never-ending and never complete. Absorbing the feminine, the 'inner woman', is but the first stage in Rilkean, alchemical 'heart-work'. For him, art is bound up with women's mysteries, so that making art is like giving birth, a connection he makes time after time in his poetry, and occasionally in his letters: 'The deepest experience of the creative artist is feminine, for it is an experience of conceiving and giving birth'. [13] One often hears artists speaking of their latest work as 'my baby'. Men here are taking over an area of women's mysteries which they know to be incredibly powerful: theologians such as St Augustine, recognizing this power, denied and hated it with a visceral vehemence. Rilke displays a jealousy of the female artist at times: for him, a creative woman was a richer and more spiritual thing than a creative male. [14] Men know that creating from one's body is infinitely more creative than creating an artwork. So we see Rilke giving birth in poems such as the second sonnet of Part One of the *Sonnets To Orpheus,* trying to incorporate the feminine into his life:

> And slept in me. Her sleep was everything:
> the awesome trees, the distances I had felt
> so deeply that I could touch them, meadows in spring:
> all wonders that had ever seized my heart.
>
> She slept the world. (Mit, 228-9)

RILKE

Rainer Maria Rilke, in true, Jungian fashion acknowledged the duality of his psyche, the masculine and feminine, light and dark, inner and outer, and so on. He attempts to integrate the feminine by making it conscious, by working it through in poems, which become self-aware 'heart-work' (Freudian dream-work). Rilke's aim is unity, integration, the union of body and soul, or, in contemporary terminology, left and right brain, of text and desire. Rilke's problem is his difficulty in handling human beings – in their fullest, fleshiest, contradictory, powerful form. He shies away from the human condition. He complains about his body; he wants to transcend the human condition, while at the same time he proposes going deeper into it, by living deeper and more painfully. These ambiguities/ confusions are expressed everywhere in his work: the desire to transcend the flesh and yet to make the experience of it even more acute; the drive towards asceticism and celibacy is counteracted by his propensity for sensuality. So in a letter, he writes

> on my return from immersion in things and animals... lo and behold! the next but one, the Angelic was set before me: so I've skipped over humanity. [15]

This is precisely Rainer Maria Rilke's problem, and the problem with Rilke: the urge to transcend humanity, the very things that make humans so beautiful, so stupid, frustrating, boring, painful, depressing, magical and ecstatic.

Rainer Maria Rilke's sexual ambivalence is expressed in his poetry by an urge towards the androgynous experience. The ultimate human being for Rilke would be a combination of male and female powers, a hermaphrodite figure which makes love to itself, in narcissistic fashion. Rilke's poetry is a mirror for his own obsessions (as is most poetry). In his poesie, he sees reflected his desires and needs, his ideas and deeds, but as highly controlled by art as is possible. The Angel is multi-sexed and multi-sexual; the blurring of gender is a powerful tendency in Rilke's poetics: while maintaining clearly defined gender roles on the one hand (woman as mother, artist, Goddess, for instance, and man as spiritual knight, philosopher, politician), Rilke also seek to blue them. He creates personages who combine genders: the Angel, Orpheus, Buddha, the dancer, the rose – these are formed of both sexes. In a letter, Rilke writes:

> perhaps the sexes are more akin than we suppose, and the great renewal of the world will perhaps consist in this, that man and maiden, freed from all false feelings and perversions, will seek each other not as opposites but as brother and sister, as neighbours, and will unite as human beings to bear in common, simply, seriously and patiently, the heavy sex that has been laid upon them. (LYP, 23)

In Rainer Maria Rilke's poetics, sex(uality) is a burden laid on humans which they have to bear as well as possible. In using the brother/ sister myth of incest, Rilke activates again the alchemical dimension, where sulphur and mercury, the King and Queen, brother and sister unite to form the androgynous being, the Magickal Child. In Rilke's art, the most majestic creation of an alchemical personage occurs in the Angel and the Buddha poems, the most exalted of which is undoubtedly 'Buddha In Glory' ('Buddha In der Glorie'), which ends the *New Poems*:

> Mitte aller Mitten, Kern der Kerne,
> Mandel, die sich einschließt und versüßt, –
> dieses alles bis an alle Sterne
> ist dein Fruchtfleisch: Sei gegrühßt.
>
> Sieh, du fühlst, wie nichts mehr an die hängt;
> im Unendlichen ist deine Schale,
> und dort steht der starke Saft und drängt.
> und von außen hilft ihm ein Gestrahle,
>
> denn ganz oben werden deine Sonnen

RILKE

voll und glühend umgedrehlt.
Doch in dir ist schon begonnen,
was die Sonnen übersteht.

(Centre of all centres, core of cores,
almost self-enclosed and growing sweet –
from all this cosmos to all the stars,
is your flesh, your fruit.

Now you feel how nothing clings to you,
your vast shell reaches into infinity,
and there the rich, thick fluids rise and flow,
illuminated in your endless peace,

those many suns of yours go spinning,
full and glowing up high.
But in you is the presence beginning
that will outlast the suns.) (Mit, 69; NP, 295)

In 'Buddha In Glory', we find one of Rainer Maria Rilke's most fervent affirmations of life. It is an affirmation, though, of inward life, the life that blossoms in the core of a fruit. Rilke loves life, but only in that dark space inside him. This is the fragment of an 'Elegy', where he says:

Let no one say that I don't love life, the eternal
presence: I pulsate in her; she bears me, she gives me
the spaciousness of this day, the primeval workday
for me to make use of... (Mit, 215)

Not for Rainer Maria Rilke the fully-fledged, fleshly lovemaking of the Greek epigrammatists, mediæval troubadours, Elizabethans or Romantic poets. Sex in Rilke's work is an ethereal kind of non-contact, if it occurs at all. He wants to transcend love. He wants a different kind of intimacy. Instead of spending hours in the love-bed, he would rather while away many days in a monastery, or a Russian *dacha,* or a Parisian garret, or some Swiss lakeside.

RILKE

Throughout the *Duino Elegies*, Rainer Maria Rilke criticizes, erases, implores and commands his lovers. He commands them to be an Angel; he begs them to transcend their self-centredness, their frustrating concentration on the love object, their narrow-mindedness. In the 'Second Elegy' of the *Duino Elegies*, Rilke describes how good lovers could be, if only... if only they could transcend themselves:

> Lovers, if they knew how, might speak wondrously
> under the night's silent air...
> It is as though all things concealed us...
> Lovers: you who suffice for each other might answer
> questions about us. You clasp one another...what's your authority?
> ...it is you that I ask about us. I know
> why your touching's so fervent: those caresses preserve!
> You safeguard forever the spot which your gentle hands cover
> and, beating beneath, you feel the true pulse of permanence...
> so that every embrace is almost to promise: Forever! (DE/C, 28-31)

Rainer Maria Rilke seems jealous of lovers here, of the contact they share: envious, most of all, of the lovers' self-sufficiency. They don't need God, or art. Lovers create a whole world, as Anaïs Nin says, and they live in it. Rilke is mad at them: don't you want *more* than that? he asks. Jealously, he prowls around like the panther in his poem.

In Rainer Maria Rilke's art, one must let go of all ballast (the imprecation in André Gide's *The Fruits of the Earth* was exactly the same: let go all your heaviness). The ballast, in the work of Rilke as in Gide, is desire:

> All things want to fly. Only *we* are weighed down by desire...
> (*Sonnets To Orpheus*, II. 14)

Looking at Paul Cézanne's paintings, Rainer Maria Rilke realized, he claimed, that it is necessary 'to go beyond even love'. [16] Again, in a letter to Xaver Kappus (May 14, 1904), Rilke states that love is a means to transcendence, but nothing more:

> Love does not at first mean merging, surrounding, and uniting with another person… Rather, it is a high inducement for the individual to ripen, to become something in himself, to become world, to become world in himself for another's sake. (In Mit, 306-7)

The poems in *Neue Gedichte* come closest to a traditional love poem ('Love Song' and 'Sacrifice', for instance), where love is conceived as the meetings of two souls, in the time-honoured Neo-platonic tradition. In the letters, Rilke makes deep connect-ions between love and death, desire and transcendence. It is typical of Rilke to write the following:

> Renunciation of love or fulfilment in love: both are wonderful and beyond compare only where the entire love-experience, with all its barely differentiable ecstasies, is allowed to occupy a central position: there (in the rapture of a few lovers or saints of *all* times and *all* religions) renunciation and completion are identical. (Letter to Rudolf Bodländer, March 23, 1922, in Mit, 339).

As in Buddhism, transcendence in Rainer Maria Rilke's art only occurs when desire has been negated. This is Rilke's way: to arrive at where he is, as Lawrence Durrell put it in a poem, through a 'series of negatives' ('I move through many negatives to what I am'). The way is thru absence, from absence thru presence to the essence. The cost in Rilke's negative mysticism is to have no family, no children, no responsibilities, no home, no job, no possessions: the life of an eternal outsider.

Rainer Maria Rilke's poetics adheres to the power of unrequited love, a love based on lack and desire, rather than consummation. This is the message of the *Duino Elegies*: 'is it not time', the narrator asks, 'that, in loving, we freed ourselves from the loved one, and, quivering, endured' (DE/L, 27). The problem for lovers, Rilke claims, is that love distracts one from achieving infinity, from moving out into the dark spaces. The problem is the relation between lovers, because Rilke believes that

> Nirgends, Geliebte, wird Welt sein als innen.
> (Nowhere, beloved can world exist but within. [DE/L, 71])

And so the traditional, romantic, Western love relationship must be dispensed with, in favour of an openness to the dark spaces. Rilke was fascinated by the person who was in love, especially the woman in love, and he wrote a number of poems on this theme. Instead of concentrating on the beloved, Rilke focusses on the person who loves; it's the same with love poets from many eras: Dante Alighieri, Francesco Petrarch, the troubadours, John Donne, William Shakespeare – they wrote of themselves, using the beloved as a pretext for emotional self-analyses. Rilke, in poems such as 'Woman In Love', brought in his notion of how love can open up the lover to the dark void: 'my heart/ seems so immense', says the woman (NP, 265).

Rainer Maria Rilke is not wholly against love: he wrote one or two lyrics which celebrate romantic, bourgeois, Western love in a fashion that is instantly recognizable:

> I long for you. To you I glide
> And lose myself – for I belong to you

says the narrator of 'The Woman Who Loves' (LP, 32). Poems such as 'Love's Beginning', which speaks of 'the ecstatic future in our faces' (P/ 26, 211), and 'Love Song', Rilke's most conventional and successful love poems, demonstrates that Rilke when he wished could exalt traditional forms of love.

Love in Rainer Maria Rilke's art is a muted, delicate affair, though not without its moments of rapture. In a letter to Lou Andreas-Salomé, Rilke describes his ideal love relationship:

RILKE

> It is not enough for two people to recognize each other, it is enormously important for them to find each other at the right time and celebrate together deep and quiet festivals in which they can grow together in their desires. [19]

In his life as much as in his poetry, Rainer Maria Rilke shows how difficult it is to achieve (and sustain) such a deep relationship. The result of pure love is forever, problematical. In his *Letters To a Young Poet*, Rilke wrote:

> Anyone who considers it seriously will find that for difficult love, as for death, which is difficult, no explanation, no solution, neither sign nor path has yet been made known. (LYP, 33)

Rainer Maria Rilke the poet offers nothing much in the way of guides or signs, apart from a belief in going beyond love. (Why? Because artists raise questions, but seldom if ever come up with all the answers. They can criticize and deconstruct society and the world, but they can't suggest what would replace it, either as an alternative society, or a utopia.)

Sexuality is sensuality in Rainer Maria Rilke's poetry – not just in his subjects – the caresses in 'Leda', or the rippling, furry torso in 'Archaic Torso of Apollo' – but also in his language, his style, his synæsthetic approach to lyrical poetry. In 1915, Rilke wrote seven phallic poems, the *Sieben Gedichte*. These might seem out of place with the rest of Rilke's restrained, suppressed/repressed sense of sexuality, but in fact it is quite a normal thing among male artists. After all, Pierre Renoir (or was it Pissarro?) said he painted with his penis; Richard Wagner (or was it Ludwig van Beethoven?) said he composed with his member; Eric Gill drew his penis, complete with measurements; while D.H. Lawrence proposed a phallic cult. Lawrence spoke of 'phallic angels', phallic religion, phallic animals (the horse, snake, tortoise, etc). The 'river-god of the blood' which appears in the 'Third Elegy' corresponds with Lawrence's cult of the 'river of blood' which joins people together during sex. In Rilke's phallic poems, the phallus is praised as a god: the Resurrection or rebirth is associated with the rising of the penis, just as in Lawrence's late work *The Escaped Cock*. [20] Lou Andreas-Salomé had already diagnosed Rilke's condition as compensation for his 'inadequacies in the erotic relation to the sex-object'. [21] In one sense, all love poetry is compensation – ultimately, love poetry is compensation for life not living up to the promise of love. Being in love produces an elation that is dissipated in everyday, workaday life. Love poetry comes out of, among other things, the gulf between being in love and being in life. Love is bliss, as all love poems state: it is also pain, hate, disgust, distance, etc. What we return to in Rilke's work, as so often, is not to a bedrock of love, or spirituality, or religion, or being, but to art.

In April, 1903, Rilke wrote:

> And in fact, artistic experience lies so incredibly near to sexual experience, to its pain and its delight, that both phenomena are really only different forms of one and the same yearning and joy. [22]

When the pleasures of art and love are equated, as here, it is clear which Rainer Maria Rilke prefers overall. In art at least, some degree of shape, pattern, imagery, style and form. Rilke prefers art to love because art needs no Other, where love, to be authentic socially and valuable psychologically, requires two people. In art, the Rilke-poet is free to love, to make love to the subjects of his poetry. Rather than observing objects/ subjects coolly and objectively, in the manner of Paul Cézanne, Rilke makes love to them, as Vincent van Gogh does. Thus he writes in *Worpswede*:

> All art is this: love, which has been poured out over enigmas – and all works of art are enigmas surrounded, adorned, enveloped by love. (In R, 98)

SIX

SYMBOLS

> It is also necessary not to lose sight of one characteristic which is specific to a symbol: its *multivalence,* which is to say the multiplicity of meanings which it expresses simultaneously. This is why it is sometimes difficult to explain a symbol, to exhaust its significations; it refers to a plurality of contexts and it is valuable on a number of levels.
>
> Mircea Eliade, *Symbolism, the Sacred and the Arts* (6)

Rainer Maria Rilke employs a number of traditional, poetic symbols in his art: the heart, the rose, the mirror, the statue, the tree, the flower, the dancer, and so on. There are a few symbols, or motifs, which Rilke has refined and personalized: the rose, the Angel, Orpheus, the sculpture and the dancer. All of Rilke's personalized symbols have a powerful spatial component. Rilke is not much concerned with colour, though if he does mention colour, it is usually the three symbolic colours of alchemy; black, white and red. Instead, Rilke speaks much of light and dark, of darkness having a radiance – in his pervasive motif of the Night (again, an ancient symbol). The Angel, too, is not a new poetic symbol or image, for it has been in use, in one form or another, for thousands of years, but Rilke gives it his own special gloss. The dancer and the sculpture set space alight, as we have noted, and engage the poet at a deep level with the urge outwards, opening onto the dark void. They are used at their most potent in the *New Poems* and the *Sonnets To Orpheus*.

Among the most powerful of Rainer Maria Rilke's symbols are those such as the rose, flowers and trees. In the *Sonnets To Orpheus*, the tree of poetry dominates the sequence as much as the girl dancer or Orpheus himself. The tree in Rilke's poetics is a soaring emblem of transcendence: this is the function of the tree in much of symbolism, to connect heaven and earth, to be the *axis mundi*, a symbol of life itself, the Cosmic Tree. The tree for Rilke forms a bridge between this world and the outer world of the dark, wild spaces, which are themselves a mirror of the interior, dark spaces.

So in the poem 'O Lacrimosa', Rilke writes:

> It is nothing but a breath, the void.
> And that green fulfilment
> of blossoming trees: a breath. (Mit, 273)

Here is the central element in Rainer Maria Rilke's vegetative symbolism: blossoming and decaying, the mythology of growth and death embodied in the tree, the plant, the flower. So much of Rilke's poetry concerns fruit and flowers, because he is always focussed on ripening, with an urge towards blossoming spatially (= spiritually). The fruit blooms in one's mouth and in one's world, in the landscape. Fruit and trees are marvellous things, says Rilke, because their continual blossoming humbles and astonishes (sonnet II.17). In sonnet I.15 of *Sonnets To Orpheus*, the proposal is to turn the whole world into a fruit:

RILKE

Tanz die Orange. Die wärmere Landschaft,
werft sie aus euch, daß die reife erstrahle
in Lüften der Heimat! Erglühte, enthüllt

Düfte um Düfte. Schafft die Verwandtschaft
mit der reinen, sich weigernden Schale,
mit dem Saft, der die Glückliche füllt!

(Dance the orange. The warmer landscape, throw it
from you, that the ripeness shines in the breezes of home!
Aglow, disclosing aroma on aroma.

Create the kin-shape with the pure,
the reluctant rine, with the juice
which fills the fortunate thing! [Mood, 66])

Of all of Rainer Maria Rilke's symbols, perhaps the rose is one of his most revered. The rose symbol neatly summarizes all of Rilke's symbolic motifs. It is a symbol found throughout his poetry. Critics typically finish up their studies with some musings on the meaning of Rilke's epitaph, where roses are noted. But that is but one of Rilke's many uses of the poetic rose. In his life, Rilke adored roses: he tended a rosebed at Muzot, and published a late work, *Les Roses*, twenty-four rose poems. [1] He sent a copy of Johannes Wolfgang von Goethe's letters to Merline with the 'sublime passages' marked with rose petals. [2] In his younger days, he slept with rose petals on his eyelids.

The rose, like the tree, the snake or the moon, is a multivalent symbol, a focal point for a plethora of meanings, among them being: the heart, grace, passion, perfection, the *unio mystica*, the mystical rose, the Goddess (the Virgin and Venus, for instance), blood, transformation, paradise, purity, death, etc. For Rilke, the rose is a symbol of transmutation, embodying so sweetly and piquantly the blossoming and decaying of life. In the rose, life and death exist at the same time. Rilke's rose is not Dante Alighieri's Mystic Rose, for death is as much a part of it as life (and, in his own life, the rose was an indicator of his death, when he pricked his finger on a thorn. [3])

In a letter, Rilke wrote:

> Everyday when I look at these beautiful white roses I ask myself whether they are not the most perfect image of this unity, I would even say this identity, of absence and presence which, perhaps, constitutes the fundamental equation of our life. (*Briefe II, 1914-26*, 374)

In the rose, Rainer Maria Rilke sees the unity of life and death, for the rose so gloriously embodies absence and presence, the death that is present even as a living thing blossoms. This is the meaning of his epitaph, this very simple but, even so, utterly extraordinary and bewildering truth: that life *and* death are present in everything. It is the kind of statement that seems to be so simplistic to some people, yet poets are fascinated and awed by such things.

In some poems, Rainer Maria Rilke employed flowers much as Dutch painters of the Golden Age did: as still-lives: Rilke then made a poem of the flowers as the painters made a painting. In this fashion, in the *Neue Gedichte*, the flowers are not used for their symbolism, but for their presence, their presence in front of the poet as he tries to describe them. This approach is found in flowerpieces such as 'Blue Hydrangea', 'The Bowl of Roses' and 'Wild Rosebush'. In one of the seven phallic poems, the rose is associated with the penis is a rather trite way, in one of Rilke's weakest lines: 'while gathering roses,/ she clasps the full body of his vital part' (P/ 26, 215). In other poems, the rose expands and takes on the full weight of symbolism. Its fragrance breathes out to fill a room, just as the Orphic poet's song breathes out to fill the space inside her/ him. Probably Rilke's two finest rose poems are 'The Bowl of Roses' and 'The Rose-Interior'. Both poems are in the *New Poems* collection, and are meditations on time, eternity and Rilkean innerness. 'The Rose-Interior' is one of those short pieces that suggest so much without being specific, without preaching or explaining, that Rilke was so good at; the poem remains a mystery to the end, like its subject, the roses:

> Welche Himmel spiegeln sich drinnen
> in dem Binnensee...
> Sie können sich selber kaum
> halten; viele leißen
> sich überfullen und fließen
> über von Innenraum
> in die Tage, die immer
> voller und voller sich schließen,
> bis der ganze Sommer ein Zimmer
> wird, ein Zimmer in einem Traum.
> (What heavens are reflected there
> in the inland lake of these open roses...
> They can scarcely contain
> themselves: many let themselves
> be filled to the brim and over
> flow with inner space
> into days that always
> fuller and fuller close,
> until the whole summer becomes
> a room, a room in a dream.) (RBR, 24)

Flowers set the poet dreaming (as also in 'Opium Poppy'). By letting himself be absorbed in the rose, the poet bypasses time and moves into timelessness (much as Sue Bridehead does for a moment in *Jude the Obscure* by Thomas Hardy, when she contemplates the flowers). For Rilke, the rose can be timeless precisely because it embodies life and death in the same moment. The rose is thus mystical, it offers a way into the mystical moment which is timeless and blissful. And when Rilke employs the rose poetically it is this meaning he goes for, over and above all the other multitudinous meanings and rose possesses.

The rose takes Rainer Maria Rilke within in a deep and illuminative fashion: so, at the end of the poem 'The Bowl of

Roses', a poem which balances a tendency towards essence-finding through presence with a Cézanne-like depiction of roses in a bowl. The final stanza, though, becomes wholly metaphysical, as the poet explores the relation between time and the rose, between his identification with the rose and its identification with the life-and-death process. The rose is the poet's self, dissolving into innerness. The rose is not a 'heap of broken images', nor a 'handful of dust': the rose embodies the pain of living that Rilke thought so important for life to be authentic. The rose is all transitoriness, yet its presence makes absence manifest and thus is for Rilke the perfect image of the transmutations of life. In the last stanza of 'The Bowl of Roses', he wrote:

> And are not all just that, just self-containing,
> if self-containing means: to take the world
> and wind and rain and patience of the spring-time
> and guilt and restlessness and muffled fate
> and sombreness of evening earth and even
> the melting, fleeing, forming of the clouds
> and the vague influence of distant stars,
> and change it to a handful of Within?
>
> It now lies heedless in those open roses. (NP, 156-9)

SEVEN

CONCLUSION

Sufferings, then, above all, the hardness of life,
the long experience of love; in fact,
purely untellable things. But later,
under the stars, what use? the more deeply untellable stars?

Rainer Maria Rilke, *Duino Elegies* (DE/L, 85)

To conclude: what has Rainer Maria Rilke's contribution to poetry been? Above all, he is a supremely lyrical, formally powerful poet. Without this syntactic magic, he would be far less influential and highly regarded. Rilke's contribution is ultimately poetic: that is, whatever he has to offer in terms of philosophy or mysticism is always pushed through to us via the medium of poetry, or what we might call 'word magic'.

In poems such as 'The Bowl of Roses', 'Orpheus. Eurydice. Hermes', 'Archaic Torso of Apollo', 'The Panther', 'The Rose-Interior', 'Before Summer Rain' and all of the *Duino Elegies* and the *Sonnets To Orpheus,* Rainer Maria Rilke shows himself to be a marvellous word magician, a shamanic force whose poetry is as magical as that of Prospero or Orpheus. In purely lyrical terms, as a maker of pure poetry, Rilke can be set alongside poets such as Sappho, Francesco Petrarch, William Shakespeare, Johann Wolfgang von Goethe, Alexander Pushkin and Torquato Tasso. In passages such as the praise to the Night in the 'Seven Elegy', Rilke burns as brightly as any poet.

I've noted that Rainer Maria Rilke is part of the German lyric tradition, and one sees this immediately if one looks at the work of Heinrich Heine, for instance, especially when he speaks of the black sun in 'Castaway':

> O you black sun, how often
> Deliciously often, I drank from you
> The wild flames of enthusiasm... (58)

Or even more acutely one sees the influence of Rainer Maria Rilke's beloved Friedrich Hölderlin, in poems such as Hölderlin's 'Bread and Wine', which Rilke used to recite: [1]

> Pealed bells are sounding quietly in the twilight air
> and a watchman mindful of the hours is calling out their number.
> Now there is a dream, which moves the tree tops in the wood,
> and look! now the shadow image of our earth, the moon,
> is on her way in secret too;
> night the dream-laden, is coming;
> full of stars, it seems, little concerned with us,
> the astonishing one, the stranger among humans
> is gleaming forth sadly and splendidly up over the mountain-tops.
> (In L. Forster, 293-4)

In the poetry of Friedrich Hölderlin, we see that grand, mythical manner which reaches out into the cosmos, in the night, into the constellations of stars, and stirs them up with yearning; that lyrical soaring of word magic which is so familiar in Romanticism, and which Rilke employed to great effect. In Romantic culture, one finds the seeds of Rilke's art and thought:

RILKE

Novalis's work especially has many correspondences. For instance, Novalis spoke of the inner life in a way which concords with Rilke's theory of innerness:

> Toward the interior goes the arcane way, in us, or nowhere, is the Eternal with its worlds, the past and future... the seat of the soul is there, where the inner world and the outer world touch [...] The inner world is... so heartfelt, so private – man is given fullness in that life – it is no native. A pity that it is so dream-like, so precarious. (*Pollen and Fragments*, 26-27, 121)

One could find correspondences with Rainer Maria Rilke's thought in all kinds of places, but the German poets and philosophers of the Romantic era and afterwards combine a particular sense of fatalism and melancholy, a subjectivity that is so intense, and a feeling for art's magic that one does not find elsewhere in quite the same mixture. We can see in Rilke's art that Buddhist resignation and humility that some think of as pessimism, which characterizes the philosophy of Arthur Schopenhauer. The links with Friedrich Nietzsche are more obvious; at the same time, Rilke is as prone to the idealism of Immanuel Kant as he is the Dionysian fervour of Nietzsche. Going further back into German history, we can find links to the mystics and poets of earlier eras, such as Angelus Silensius, who said:

> Time is as Eternity, and Eternity as Time only if you yourself make no difference between them. (In L. Forster, 143)

Much of Rainer Maria Rilke's poetry concerns abolishing time, or with subsuming past, present and future within the self, so that they become one, or so that the self can transcend time altogether. The *Duino Elegies* in particular look towards a space which is beyond time. The timeless moment is a deep concern of mystics, but most poets of the modern era have written of timelessness in one way or another: T.S. Eliot, Robert Graves,

RILKE

Arthur Rimbaud, Georg Trakl, Octavio Paz, Robert Frost, Gertrude Stein, Emily Dickinson, Marina Tsvetayeva, C.P. Cavafy, etc. Rilke is by no means alone in his exploration of spiritual issues. There are so many major poets who tackle the spiritual dimension in poetry; apart from the poets noted above, one might also include Juan Ramón Jiménez, Pablo Neruda, George Seferis, Umberto Saba, Sylvia Plath, Adrienne Rich, Kathleen Raine, Osip Mandelstam, Fyodor Tyutchev, Eugenio Montale, Paul Celan, Cesare Pavese, Dino Campana and St-John Perse.

One of the hallmarks of Rainer Maria Rilke's spiritual/ transcendent poetry is its restlessness. The *Duino Elegies* froth with poetic energy, with a variety of spiritual crises and ontological doubts. J.P. Stern wrote (in *The Heart of Europe*):

> If there is one theme which German poets of the last three centuries have made peculiarly and poignantly their own, it is their concern with the world as a place of insecurity and impermanence, a provisional state... [2]

This Existential restlessness (or uncertainty) is a major component of the work of German philosophers and writers such as Franz Kafka, Robert Musil, Karl Kraus, Georg Trakl, Ludwig Wittgenstein, Friedrich Nietzsche and Arthur Schopenhauer. All of Rilke's symbols and themes are marked by flux and ambiguity: the Angel, the dancer, Orpheus, the void, death, solitude, love, the rose, the tree. Transformation is a primary theme in Rilke's poetics, and in the *Sonnets To Orpheus* we read lines such as:

> 'Words still melt into something beyond their embrace' (II.10.14);
> 'Choose to be changed' (II.12.1);
> 'Dancer: you transmutation
> of all going-by into going: what you have wrought!' (II.18.1-2)

RILKE

We have placed Rainer Maria Rilke within the mystical tradition because Rilke targets the zones of mysticism: the urge for unity, the desire for pure being, the asceticism required for contemplation, the need for an experience of timelessness and bliss, the dissolution of duality, the yearning for reaching to the essence of things. Mystics of all ages have stressed the need to find the essence of things and then to embrace it. The essence has several names: Allah, Tao, Logos, Jehovah, Buddha, Krishna, Brahma, God, the One, the All, Spirit, etc. But there is everywhere the same need for deep contact with something that is supermeaningful. The means differ – sensual overload or harsh asceticism, etc – but the end is similar. The degree to which mystics experience the goal differs – Sufi mystics dissolve in Allah like a moth in a flame, while Catholic unite with God as lovers, in an erotic fashion. The terminology differs; the props of mysticism differ; the expressions in prose and poetry differ; the ethics differ; the metaphysics differ; the cultural contexts differ; but the ultimate aims – to come close to the Ultimate – are similar. This is not to say that all forms of mysticism are the same or that their goals are the same, but that they share many elements in common. Among the most crucial of which is the need for some kind of deep contact with something thought or felt to be hugely important, what we could call the 'supermeaningful'.

In Rainer Maria Rilke's poetics, the mystical urge veers between imagination (in art) and wishing (in dream or unconscious imagery); between actuality in art, and possibility in life. Rilke's art is half-dream, half-reality; in other words, he only goes so far in trying to achieve his ontological aims. He knows that much can be attained in art, but that it is, ultimately, useless unless it can be integrated into life. This is why the woman artist is so much more powerful and so much more successful for Rilke: because she can create *in life* as well as in art. The female artist can really be creative in life, whereas the male artist can't quite be so creative. The female artist goes further than the male artist for Rilke: she can soar and dive deep, while the male artist cannot travel or reach the same places (all of this, of course, occurs if we follow Rilke's modernist poetics, via second wave feminism, and a biologist and essentialist view of humanity and creativity. Many theorists have debunked any philosophy founded in biology or essentialism).

Anyway, to continue: Rainer Maria Rilke tried to explore what second wave feminists have called the 'wild zone' of women: men have their own 'wild zone', known from art and legend, the realm of hunting, aggression, brotherhood, etc, the wildness which exists at the edge of culture. Women have their own 'wild zone', too, according to some second wave feminists, but this is largely unknown to men. [3] Rilke, like D.H. Lawrence, tried to venture into the female 'wild zone', with his poetry of dark spaces, but he couldn't go as far into that place as the female artist. The female artist, in Rilke's view, is closer to the Earth, to birth, flesh, growth, nature, etc, and at the same time, is wilder, more creative, and closer to the Angels.

Rainer Maria Rilke's poetry is not all dreaming, but its success is largely poetic. That is, the transformation in Rilke's art are poetic, not actual: poetry is dream-work, in the Freudian manner, as well as magic in the occult manner, and pleasure in the social realm. The poet sees the lack of fulfilment in life, and transfers it to the world of poetry; the poem then reflects back its magic into the poet's life, and into the world. Poetry is therefore transformation material, a way of altering one's life, and the life of the consumer. Sigmund Freud saw this kind of dream-work as the working out of desire: for Freud, desire lies at the foundations of art. In his *The Interpretation of Dreams*, Freud wrote:

> Thought is after all nothing but a substitute for a hallucinatory wish; and it is self-evident that dreams must be wish-fulfilments, since nothing but a wish can set our mental apparatus at work. [4]

RILKE

In the Freudian view, the world is founded on wish or desire, and much of poetry is wishing. Desire not only powers love poetry, but also Rainer Maria Rilke's kind of poetry, which aims for the evocation of states of being which are largely beyond the grasp of language. As a shaman, the poet wishes to control and shape the outside world by transforming the inner world. Rilke is a shamanic poet in this respect: in magic, the tenet 'as above, so below' is turned, in the modern era, to mean 'as outside so inside'. And vice versa. In other words, by transforming the inner realms, the outer world becomes transformed. (As filmmaker Jean-Luc Godard put it, how do you show the inside? By remaining resolutely outside).

Like the child, the magician believes that the world revolves around her/ him: the world is a reflection of her/ himself. Thus, in the poetry of Rilke, we see the desire to make the world in the poet's image, to turn the dark, wild spaces he finds inside himself into the world outside. Conversely, the wild, dark voids the poet keeps describing are the manifestations of the poet's own inner states. This is the thrust of much of Rilke's poesie, particularly the *Duino Elegies*:

> But, oh, the nights – those nights when the Infinite wind
> eats at our faces! Who is immune to the night, to Night,
> ever-subtle, deceiving? Hardest of all to the lonely,
> Night, is she gentler to lovers? DE/C, 21)

The deeper and wilder the evocations of the night outside makes the inner transformation so much deeper and wilder. Rainer Maria Rilke's great contribution to poetry stems partly from this psychological nurturing of the equivalence of inner and outer, born in Symbolist thought, and given his own peculiar emphasis. What it does, mystically, is to state clearly and lyrically that *here* is the bliss space, and that *now* is the time for bliss and transformation. This is a profoundly mystical statement, and so many religions point towards it. Critics have problems with Rilke because they are unsure of his mysticism; certainly he was, as Eudo Mason states, 'beyond all question radically anti-Christian' (1938, 20). This upsets some critics: they get confused because Rilke used motifs such as angels, Madonnas, roses and other kinds of Christian symbols and images. But these motifs are only the way in which Rilke's ideas manifested themselves: they are cultural constructs which mask, as in poets such as Arthur Rimbaud and D.H. Lawrence, a more expansive, pagan, mythic vision. Christianity in Rilke's poetics is only one expression of a wider, religious sensibility. While the Angel seems a Christian symbol at first glance, it goes far beyond the Christian concept of an angel, as Rilke explained. Similarly, Orpheus not only predates Christ historically, as a mythical figure, he also surpasses Christ (for Rilke) as a pan-cosmic embodiment of the spirit and flight of poetry.

Mystically, Rainer Maria Rilke's contribution to poetry is to keep reaching for those zones of being, as Samuel Beckett called them, which lie beyond words, beyond visual representation, beyond even the senses. Rilke's synæsthesia fuses all the senses while at the same time wanting to transcend them, so that the result of his mystical poems is a dialectical movement between art an life, being and non-being, here and there, inner and outer, light and dark, desire and negation.

Again and again in his poetry, Rainer Maria Rilke emphasized the here and the now. In the *Elegies*, this theme becomes stridently expressed:

> O Mädchen,
> dies: daß wie liebten in uns, nicht Eines, ein Künftiges, sondern
> das zahllos Braudende...
> Und waren doch in unserem Alleingehn
> mit Dauserndem...

RILKE

Hier ist des Säglichen Zeit, hier seine Heimat.
Sprich und bekenn.

> (O maiden,
> *this*: that we've loved, *within* us, not one, still to come, but all
> the innumerable fermentation ...
> Yet, when alone, we entertain ourselves
> with everlastingness...
> *Here* is the time for the *sayable, here* is its homeland.
> Speak and bear witness.)
> (DE/L, 45, 53; Mit, 201)

Rainer Maria Rilke is at his wildest and, for some critics, his most improbable when he comes out with statements of pure life affirmation, as in:

Hier ist Magie (here is magic, P/26, 321)
Hiersein ist herrlich (being here is glorious, DE/L, 71)
Gesang ist dasein (song is existence, Mit, 231)

At these moments, Rainer Maria Rilke's poetry becomes wholly mystical, wholly in tune with Taoism, with archaic shamanism, with Buddhism, with the Australian aborigines' *alchuringa* dreamtime. These mystical statements are offensive to some non-poets. Being here is glorious – children and artists understand this. It is not something easily put into words, either, although that is the poet's job, and the poet's never-ending problem. As Chuang-tzu said:

Tao is something beyond material existences. It cannot be conveyed either by words or by silences. [5]

Poetry cannot fully resolve such paradoxes, but it can get closer than most prose. Sculpture might be a better way, and in many poems Rainer Maria Rilke tried to approach the condition of sculpture. Rilke, like Arthur Rimbaud, Robert Graves, Gertrude Stein, Anaïs Nin, Aldous Huxley and Hermann Hesse, would agree with Bertrand Russell when he said he was a 'dissenter from all known religions'. [6] Yet poets such as Rimbaud, Graves, Samuel Beckett and Marina Tsvetayeva are profoundly religious – both in their outlook and in their art. This is something that critics find very hard to comprehend (or they resist it), yet poets find it all quite natural.

Poetry is is the revelation, criticism is the mopping up afterwards. Poets seldom explain their art to everyone's satisfaction. Despite writing so many letters, Rilke did not, like Dante Alighieri in the *Vita Nuova* (*New Life*), offer up a prose commentary on his poems. While a poet such as Samuel Beckett kept quiet about art (usually), Rilke often spoke of art; but his philosophy of art has to be pieced together from the letters, one or two essays, *The Rodin Book*, and the poems themselves. The poetry is central, and constitutes the revelation of art. It is the same with Zen Buddhism, as Alan Watts said in *The Way of Zen*:

> For Zen spoils neither the æsthetic shock nor the *satori* shock by filling in, by explanation, second thoughts, and intellectual commentary. (1962, 220)

We are back here with the central precept of the *Tao Te Ching*, which is:

> One who knows does not speak; one who speaks does not know. (117)

The artist is stuck in a curious position: what s/he wants to engage – love, death, being – are zones of experience beyond the reach of language. Yet s/he must speak, must create. This is a dilemma that all poets face. Samuel Beckett could not resolve the desire to speak with the urge not to speak: Beckett worked on this problem to the end of his life, without satisfactorily solving it. He didn't stop writing, either, thus always breaking his code of keeping silence.

RILKE

For the mystic, the problem is to find the right words to describe the mystical experience. So many mystics have been great poets – Jalal al-Din Rumi, St John of the Cross, Chuang-tzu, Hui-Neng, Sankara, etc. Poetry is thus indispensable for the mystic. Unpoetical mysticism is largely ineffective. But, mysticism is naturally poetry anyway. All mystical utterances feel poetic. The poet's job in the realm of mysticism is thus to say as much as possible in as few words as possible. To speak, as it were, without speaking.

This is why the language of negativity works so well in the poetry of mysticism, the 'not-this-not-that' of Oriental mysticism, the 'from nothing to nothing' of Meister Eckhart. Absence flips over to indicate presence. This is Rainer Maria Rilke's poetic method. Of all mystics, he is probably closest to Eckhart – who believed that Heaven begins here, not in some other world; Eckhart maintained that the spiritual voyage returns one to the Earth, not away from it; that the way to God was the *via negativa*. Eckhart speaks, like Rilke, in terms of being, of is-ness. Eckhart wrote:

> The seed of God is in us... The seed of a pear tree grows into a pear tree, a hazel seed into a hazel tree, a seed of God into God. [8]

This view is very similar to that of Rainer Maria Rilke and many other poets. The imagery employed, of seeds and trees, is not out of place in the poetry of Arthur Rimbaud, Sappho, D.H. Lawrence or Robert Herrick. Rilke, like Lawrence, is always writing of blossoming, of expanding like a seed, of turning oneself into a seed. One merely has to change Meister Eckhart's Christian terminology: 'the seed of being is in us'. Rilke wants to explode the self into beingness, rather than into God.

There are further correspondences between Rainer Maria Rilke and Meister Eckhart: like St John of the Cross, Eckhart is a mystic who thought is close to that of Buddhism. In discussing the Zen Buddhist experience of Suchness, D.T. Suzuki says it is close to Eckhart's notion of *istikeit* or is-ness. Zen Buddhist Suchness or is-ness, Suzuki claims, is wholly beyond words:

> No words can express what it is, but as words are the only instrument given us human being to communicate our thought, we have to use words, with this caution: Nothing is available to our purpose; to say "not available"... is not to the point either. Nothing is acceptable. To say it is, is already negating itself. Suchness transcends everything, it has no moorings. No concepts can reach it, no understanding can grasp it. Therefore, it is called pure experience. (in R. Woods, 141)

Such areas of experience which are beyond words infuriate critics who like everything to be neatly mapped out, cleanly categorized. Poets, though, like mystics, deal in uncertainties, in flux, in ambiguities, in contradictions, puzzles, paradoxes, amazements. Poets fully acknowledge the unreasonableness of the world and of experience. For them, many things are beyond the reach of language, but we still have to try to grasp them. The poet's task is, artistically, a shot in the dark, a leap, as Chuang-tzu said, into the unknown. Yet most poets feel quite at home there.

Meister Eckhart spoke of the Godhead beyond God, which is similar to Sankara's notion of Brahma. [9] In a similar vein, Rainer Maria Rilke speaks of a state of beingness which is beyond the usual, traditional notions of beingness. It is to this distant realm of being that the poet wishes to go. So Rilke writes, in sonnet I.3:

> True singing is a different breath, about
> nothing. A bust inside the god. A wind. (Mit, 231)

Inside Orpheus, Rainer Maria Rilke says, is a new, different spaciousness which poetry can activate by its Orphic power of singing. The space is *inside* the god Orpheus, Rilke states, and Orpheus resembles Buddha here, and so like the Brahma of

Hinduism, the Universal Being. In the *Sonnets To Orpheus*, we see that urge in Rilke's art that is Buddhist: to transcend the personal and move into the Universal Self.

This is the meaning of the *Sonnets To Orpheus*, a feeling for transcendence which is summarized in sonnet 29 of Part Two (quoted in full above). Be, go, fly, Rilke encourages: be that void, be that glittering night of stars, be that tree of transcendence, be that dance, go to the dark spaces, fly in the scintillating void. In Rika Lesser's translation of sonnet 29, Part Two:

> Still friend of the many distances, feel
> how your breath, your breathing still enlarges Space.
> …let yourself sound, resound.
> …Give yourself to Transformation…
> be that magic power at the crossroads
> of your Senses. Be Sense, the significance
> of their Strange, their special meeting. (RBR, 58)

In this sonnet, Rainer Maria Rilke is at his most joyous. For a poet of negative mysticism one might think joy to be the last thing on his mind. In fact, it is primary. Joy abounds in the mysticisms of absence, such as Taoism, Buddhism, in Eckhartian Christianity. Of course, Rilke's kind of mystical joy is not a superficial form of happiness or self-contentment. It is the deep joy that comes from mystical being, a radiant bliss found in the ecstasies of mystics. As Rilke put it in sonnet II.8:

> When we were filled with joy.
> it belonged to no one: it was simply there. (Mit, 243)

It is also beyond words, as are most of the best things in life:

> The reality of any joy in the world is indescribable… joy is a marvellous increasing of what exists, a pure addition out of nothingness. [10]

RILKE

Joy for Rainer Maria Rilke, as for Friedrich Nietzsche, is part of the Existential intensification of the experience of being alive. This is the meaning of the 'Ninth Elegy' of the *Duino Elegies*: to experience life so deeply it becomes joyous. For Rilke, as for philosophers such as Nietzsche and Paul Tillich, pain and bliss are intertwined: one must give, says Rilke, one's 'full and *joyous* consent' to 'the dreadfulness of life' in order to 'take possession of the unutterable abundance and power of our existence'. [11] In Rilke's philosophy, as in the philosophies of Søren Kirkegaard and Jean-Paul Sartre, acts of pure faith, pure shots in the darkness, are required if living is to be fully authentic. Tillich calls this the 'courage to be', which demands nothing less than 'absolute faith':

> It is the accepting of the acceptance without somebody or something that accepts. It is the power of being-itself that accepts and gives the courage to be. [12]

For Paul Tillich, the 'courage to be' is an Existential embrace of the meaninglessness of everything, a divine acceptance. Rainer Maria Rilke moved towards this state of acceptance, but it took him a long time to reach it. After the struggle of the *Duino Elegies* comes the relative calm of the *Sonnets To Orpheus,* but the goal of beingness needed all of that struggle in order to be achieved. Even then, Rilke's grasp of beingness is shaky. In 1914, he wrote to Sidie Nadherny:

> I'm stuck in the pressure of the new beginning, which I want to do *well, well* (it can easily be ruined), what I want is a pure spiritual life, every day the same, no distractions, no claims on me, *all expectation turned inward* toward the heart where my next task must emerge. (*Briefe an Sidonie Nadherny*, 181-2)

This is the familiar Rainer Maria Rilke talking: the need for quiet and seclusion, the need to be free of societal, familial and economic responsibilities, etc; the need to concentrate on a new beginning. Artists are always going through new beginnings. Each phase, each work is a new beginning. This is Rilke's eternal problem: to prepare the space in which the fresh start can blossom. 'What's needed is just this: Loneliness, vast, inner loneliness', he wrote in 1903. [14] To clear everything out of the way so that, as he says at the end of the 'Ninth Elegy':

> Überzähliges Dasein
> entspringt mir im Herzen.
> (Supernumerous being wells up in my heart. DE/L, 89)

Rainer Maria Rilke knows, as all poets know, that:

> Aber noch ist uns das Dasein verzaubert
> (Even today, though, existence is magical)
> (SO/L, 106-7)

Here is magic; existence is magical; being here is glorious – these phrases of total affirmation seem like wild optimism until one recalls that they are commonplaces that ought to be the norm. When Rainer Maria Rilke states that 'existence is magical', he is not going off on some mad, Nietzschean, philosophical trip. He is stating, plainly, that life is magical. The question then arises: why isn't it magical all the time? This is the key problem of the human condition, according to writers such as Colin Wilson and thinkers such as Georg Gurdjieff. Wilson and Gurdjieff (and many others like them) maintain that we are only half alive most of the time. We need to *wake up*, they claim. This is all very well, and probably mostly true. The problem is, as always, *how*?

Rainer Maria Rilke could not solve the issue of how to attain pure being, but neither could other poets such as Arthur Rimbaud and William Shakespeare. Poets and mystics are pleased to tell us what being *is not*, but what it actually is, they can't really say. As the Sixth Patriarch notes, in the *T'an-ching*, a

RILKE

Chinese text:

> In this moment there is nothing which comes to be. In this moment there is nothing which ceases to be. Thus there is no birth-and-death to be brought to an end. Wherefore the absolute tranquillity in this present moment. Though it is at this moment there is no limit to this moment, and herein is eternal delight. [15]

Painters who talk too much (or paint too much) are not true painters, according to Rainer Maria Rilke (Cez, 75-76). We know what he means: the artist should focus on making art. Artists such as Mark Rothko agree: too much talk kills art, they say. Yet - poetry is all talk, all language, all words flying about trying to describe experiences that are beyond words. On this question of the relation of art to life, of language to being, the Oriental mystics have the most insight. A *haiku* poem by Gochiku says it all in a short, compact but illuminating fashion:

> The long night
>   The sound of the water
>   Says what I think. [16]

This is how art points: don't look to me, it says, look to nature, and you'll see it all laid out. His is not pantheism or the Romantic pathetic fallacy; rather, it is an opening out of consciousness. In this way, art acts like religion: it thrusts one out of oneself, into an expansive, larger, mythic, spiritual realm. The mythicizing process is how art expands awareness. Look, says the Gochiku poem above, at the water and listen to it: it embodies philosophy. Nature, says the poet, does the *real* talking. Which is of course true. However much humans prattle, nature has the final word. Whatever art may say, nature says more. You can't out-speak nature. You go back into it after death. From an eternal perspective, nature eventually absorbs all human culture.

Beyond art, then, lies nature, and also under it and all the way through it. Nature is the final wild zone (and the first). Hence Rainer Maria Rilke's use of the motif of the night: the night hangs above the Angel in the *Duino Elegies*. The night is Rilke's symbol or image for the beyond of nature that is the wild zone. When art stops, there will always be the night (nature), says Rilke. In a different but connected vein, Rilke's contemporary, Ludwig Wittgenstein, wrote in his *Philosophical Investigations:*

> Would it be imaginable that people should never speak an audible language? But still say things to themselves in the imagination? [17]

People never stop speaking, it seems, whether audibly, silently, imaginatively, or artistically. There's always a little voice yakking away somewhere. Ludwig Wittgenstein's question addresses a particular aspect of linguistics which is not Rilke's province, but it does hint at the relation between language and identity, and between language and being. Clearly, a poet such as Rilke needs language to define himself, his position in the self-world interface. He needs language too to construct that all-important bridge between himself and the dark spaces, between his self and his self-within-beingness. Without poetry, Rilke, and all poets, would not have been able to make the connections necessary for the attainment of beingness. Language molded into poetry is the basic stuff of transformation.

Rainer Maria Rilke's self-transcendence has not been through any particular religion. As with poets such as Heinrich Heine, Paul Eluard, C.P. Cavafy and Arthur Rimbaud, there are elements of Neoplatonism, Christian, Greek mythology, occultism and Western philosophy in Rilke's art. There are also elements of German idealist philosophy (Immanuel Kant and G.W.F. Hegel), of Gnosticism, and of the pre-Existentialist thinkers like Søren Kirkegaard, Arthur Schopenhauer and Friedrich Nietzsche.

But Rainer Maria Rilke's self-transcendence is not aligned

fundamentally to established religion (tho' it draws on the themes and images of it). Some critics feel the need to place Rilke's art, as with Arthur Rimbaud, within Christianity. But Rilke, like Rimbaud, is always breaking those bonds, and moving out into paganism, into Hellenism, into alchemy, into Ancient Egyptian, Greek and Roman mythology, into all kinds of arcania. Catholic theologians (such as Bernard Lonergan) claim that self-transcendence only occurs through love, through being-in-love: for theoligians such as Lonergan, 'the experience of being-in-love is an experience of fulfilment, of complete integration'. [18]

But Rainer Maria Rilke is in love with being, and God is not love but beingness in his metaphysics. Rilke's love and need for experiences such as being explains poems such as sonnet thirteen of Part Two of *Sonnets To Orpheus*, which Rilke regarded as the key poem in the *Sonnets To Orpheus* sequence. The sentiment of the poem goes beyond Christianity, and beyond paganism. In fact, Rilke creates his own cult, his own religion, as do many poets, artists, shamans (and lovers). It is a religion of darkness, music, being, space, Orphic voices, stars, roses, solitude, asceticism, sculpture, innerness and fierce deities such as the Angel. Sonnet 13 of *Sonnets To Orpheus*, Part Two, sums up Rilke's poetic religion:

> Be ahead of all farewells, as though they were already
> behind you, like the winter that has just gone by.
> For through some winter you feel such wintriness bind you,
> that only by wintering through it will your heart survive.
>
> Be dead forever in Eurydice, – more gladly arise
> into the seamless life proclaimed in your song.
> Here, in this realm of decline, among momentary days,
> be the crystal cup that shattered even as it rang.
>
> Be – and yet know the great void where all things being,
> the infinite ground of your inmost vibration,
> so that you accomplish it this one time.

RILKE

To the used-up, as well as all the muffled and dumb,
creatures within copious Nature, the unsayable sums,
count yourself joyfully among them, and cancel the count.
(SO/Y, 113; Mit, 245)

Rainer Maria Rilke's state of poetic being looks to the Orient: Rilke's brilliance is to suggest a whirlwind of constellations, nighttime and being using a web of lyricism, rhymes and carefully chosen words; to suggest the place with economic, simple language; to suggest it using the whole weight of absence. That space between the lines of a *haiku* poem is the space of Rilke's poetry: it is the nourishment of absence. Like all states of being that are mystical, it happens now. Alan Watts wrote in *The Way of Zen*:

> There is only this now. It does not come from anywhere; it is not going anywhere. It is not permanent, but it is permanent. Though moving, it is always still. (198)

For some critics, Rainer Maria Rilke had no philosophy; if there is or was no philosophy, writes Timothy J. Casey in his centenary essay, there was at least 'an existential confrontation of quite extraordinary intensity' (106). Rilke does not fit into any particular artistic movement, as Arnold Bauer noted in his 1972 study of Rilke: 'In his entire lifetime, Rilke belonged to no group or clique', [20] a view also held by Romano Guardini in *Rilke's Duino Elegies*. [21]

•

Rainer Maria Rilke's delicacy is his strength; his sense of absence is his richness; his sense of death becomes an increased feeling for life ('That is the essential: to see everything *within* life itself, even the mystical, even death' [22]); his restlessness is not much indecision as continuous ambiguity. Criticism of Rilke's art might include his narcissism – but most great poets are narcissistic

RILKE

(Petrarch, Dante, Sappho, Catullus, Rimbaud, Shakespeare). His inability to transform his life the way he did in his poetry is sometimes criticized: but how many poets have been successful in that area? (And how many critics?!). If anything, Rilke's poetry is too repetitive, always hacking away at the same problem in the same manner – in his letters as much as in his poetry. This single-mindedness is not a problem in itself – many painters do this. What happens with Rilke is that his repetition blinds him to other possibilities, to other methods, to other ways of tackling the central conundrum of being alive. But Rilke certainly got as close to his goal as most mystics, at least in the area of defining his target. And, further, he did so in superbly fluid, vivid, elegant poetry. For this reason alone, for his marvellous poetry, he is an important artist; combined with his mystical feelings, he becomes very great. Rilke foregrounds ambiguity and confusion, changeability and difficulty; he remains authentic, despite the flourishes, for he always remains humane, proud but also humble, arrogant but also flawed and pained. For these reasons (and others), we value Rilke very highly.

Rainer Maria Rilke
by Maler Helmut Westoff (above).

Rilke at the Hotel Biron, Paris (above), and in 1897 (left).

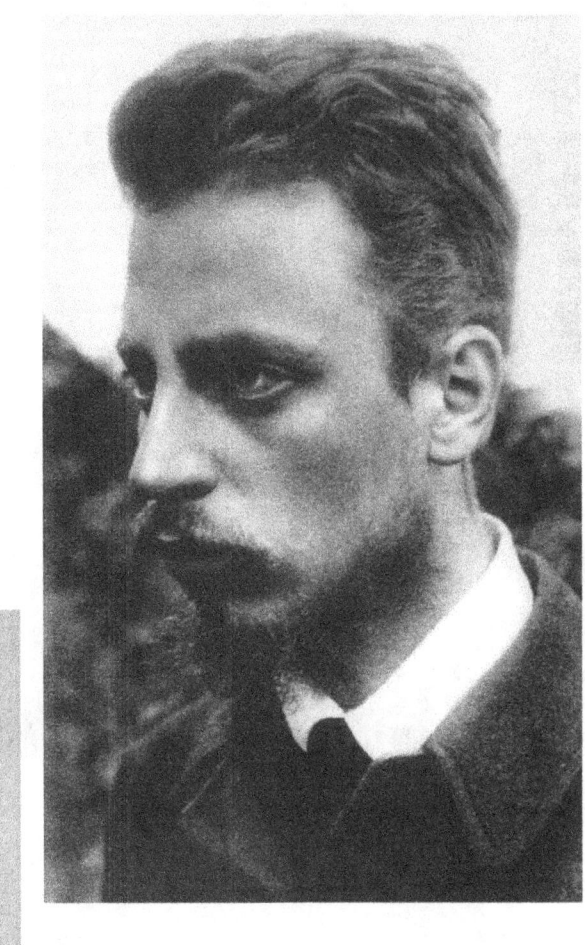

Lou Andreas-Salomé

NOTES

CHAPTER ONE: POETRY

1. Rilke, *Briefe 1906-1907*, 279.
2. G. Hughes, 60.
3. W. La Barre, *The Ghost Dance*; Ted Hughes: *Shakespeare and the Goddess of Complete Being*, Faber, 1992; J. Campbell, *The Power of Myth*; J. Ferguson, *An Illustrated Encyclopedia of Mysticism*, Thames & Hudson, 1976; R. Graves, *On English Poetry*, Heinemann, 1922.
4. R. Taylor, 28.
5. L. Wittgenstein, *Tractatus Logico-Philosophicus*.
6. P. Valéry, "Mallarmé", in *An Anthology*, 108-9.
7. Rilke, Nov 28, 1925, in H. Hollthusen, 1952, 7.
8. Y. Buson, in L. Stryk, 96.
9. M. Basho, in ib., 89.
10. M. Eliade, *Shamanism*, 391.
11. Rilke, *Poems 1906-1907*, 150.
12. Rilke, letter to Katherine Kippenberg, in Rilke/ Kippenberg, *Briefwechsel*, 685.
13. Rilke, letter, Mch 17, 1922, in *New Poems*, Introduction, 40.

CHAPTER TWO: SPACE

1. Rilke, *Briefe aus Muzot*, 334f.
2. Rilke, letter to Lotte Heinar, Nov 8, 1915, in Mit, 340.
3. Rilke, letter to Countess Margot Sizzo-Noris-Crouy, Jan 6, 1923, in Mit, 332.
4. Rilke, letter to Sizzo-Noris-Crouy, in Mit, 317.
5. Chuang-tzu, quoted in W. Johnson, *Riding the Ox Home*, Rider, 1982.
6. M. Eliade, *Patterns In Comparative Religion*, 182.

7. F. Nietzsche, *The Anti-Christ*, in *A Nietzsche Reader*, 190-1.
8. Rilke, *Briefe aus Muzot*, op. cit., 333-4.

CHAPTER THREE: ESSENCE

1. D.T. Suzuki, *The Basics of Buddhist Philosophy*, Allen & Unwin, 1957, in R. Woods, 126.
2. In W.L. Graff, 208-9.
3. M. Eliade, *Symbolism, the Sacred and the Arts*, 5-6.
4. Rilke, letter to 'une amie', Feb 3, 1923, in Mit, 299.
5. In Mit, 215.
6. Rilke and Andreas-Salomé, *Briefwechsel*, Aug 15, 1903, in Mit, 303.
7. Rilke, letter to Magda von Hattingberg, Feb 17, 1914, in *Briefwechsel mit Benventura*.
8. Rilke, *Rodin and Other Prose Poems*, 9.
9. In ib., 9.
10. Rilke, letter to Clara, Mch 8, 1907, in *Gesammalte Briefe, 1892-1926*, II, 279f.
11. Rilke, to Clara, Oct 13, 1907, in Mit, 306.
12. Rilke, letter to Nora Wydenbruck, Aug 11, 1924, in Mit, 324.
13. See Aldous Huxley, *The Perennial Philosophy*, Chatto & Windus, 1969, 8, and R. Woods, 66.
14. C.G. Jung, *Memories, Dreams and Reflections*, 414; *The Archetypes and the Collective Unconscious*, Routledge, vol. 9, 275.
15. C.G. Jung, *The Structure and Dynamics of the Psyche*, in *Memories, Dreams and Reflections*, 414.

CHAPTER FOUR: ANGELS

1. Rilke, letter, Nov 13, 1925, in DE/L, 152.
2. Walter Kaufmann, *From Shakespeare To Existentialism*, Princeton University Press, N.J., 1980, 233.
3. See K. May, *Nietzsche and Modern Literature*, 53.
4. *Pancavimca Brahmana*, in M. Eliade, *Symbolism*, 4.
5. 'Angels remind us of what we lack, and Rilke is reconciled to that we are, so to speak, the 'not-Angels'. That is exactly our state', noted Keith May, 153.
6. Rilke, *Briefe aus Muzot*, 333.
7. Rilke, letter, 1925, in Mit, 316.
8. Rilke, letter to Sizzo-Noris-Crouy, Apl 12, 1923, in Mit, 317.

9. Rilke, *Briefe an Nanny Wunderly-Volksart*, 798.
10. Rilke, letter, 1903, in DE/L, 120.

CHAPTER FIVE: GODDESS

1. Rilke, letter to Andreas-Salomé, *Briefwechsel*, 119.
2. H.F. Peters, 52.
3. F. Nietzsche, *Briefe an Peter Gast*, Leipzig, 1924, 89-90.
4. Lou Andreas-Salomé, *Lebensruckblick*, 138.
5. Rilke, letters to Andreas-Salomé, *Briefwechsel*, 250.
6. In ib., 48.
7. Rilke, *Briefe, 1907-1914*, 22.
8. Rilke, *Furstin Marie von Thurn und Taxis-Hohenlohe*, 303f.
9. W. Leppmann, *Rilke*, 79.
10. See H.F. Peters, 53f; D. Prater, 66f.
11. Lou Andreas-Salomé, *Lebensruckblick*, 146.
12. Rilke to Andreas-Salomé, Mch 1, 1912, in N. Wydenbruck, 209.
13. Rilke, letter to a 'young woman', Nov 20, 1904, in Mit, 337.
14. Rilke, letter to Hugo Holler, June 12, 1909, in *Berliner Tageblatt*, Nov 29, 1929, in Mit, 209.
15. Rilke, *Briefe, 1907-1914*, 275.
16. Rilke, letter to Clara Rilke, Oct 13, 1907, in Mit, 306.
17. Rilke, letter to Xavier Jappus, May 14, 1904, in Mit, 306-7.
18. Rilke, letter to Rudolf Bodkinder, Mch 23, 1922, in Mit, 339.
19. Rilke, letter, *Briefe, 1892-1904*, 35.
20. D.H. Lawrence, *The Escaped Cock*, in *The Complete Short Novels*, Penguin, 1985; the phallic cult of Lawrence also appears in *St Mawr*, *Lady Chatterley's Lover* and *The Plumed Serpent*, among others.
21. In Ernest Pfeiffer, *Lou Andreas-Salomé*, 285; and in D. Prater, 271.
22. Rilke, letter to Xavier Kappus, 1903, in E. Mason, 1963, 54.

CHAPTER SIX: SYMBOLS

1. See H.F. Peters, 182-3; S. Mandel, 192-7; E.M. Butler, 407.
2. See D. Prater, 320.
3. Rilke cut his hand on a rose thorn when he picked some roses from his garden for Madame Eloui Bey; the wound was slight but led to an infection 'that revealed the advanced state of leukemia', according to H.F. Peters, 186.
4. Rilke, letter, *Briefe II, 1914-26*, 374.

SEVEN: CONCLUSION

1. F. Hölderlin, in L. Forster, 293-4.
2. J.P. Stern, *The Heart of Europe*, 307.
3. See E. Showalter, "Feminist Criticism In the Wilderness", in E. Showalter, 1985; Jeanne Addison Roberts, *The Shakespearean Wild*, University of Nebraska Press, Lincoln, 1991, 2-3; Xavière Gauthier, "Why Witches?", in E. Marks, 199-203.
4. S. Freud, *The Interpretation of Dreams*, tr. J. Strachey, Penguin, 1976, 721.
5. Chuang-tzu, in *Chuang-tzu*, tr. H.A. Giles, Kelley & Walsh, Shanghai, 1926, 351.
6. B. Russell, *Bertrand Russell's Best*, Allen & Unwin, 1975, 46.
7. A. Watts, *The Way of Zen*, 220.
8. James M. Clark & John V. Skinner, *Meister Eckhart*, London, 1953, 51. See also R. Woods, 551.
9. See Rudolf Otto, *Mysticism East and West*, tr. Bracey & Payne, Macmillan, New York, 1979; and R. Woods, 428-9.
10. Rilke, letter to Isle Erdman, Jan 31, 1914, in Mit, 330.
11. Rilke, letter to Margot Sizzo-Noris-Crouy, Apl 12, 1923, in Mit, 317.
12. Paul Tillich, *The Courage To Be*, Collins, 1977, 179.
13. *Briefe an Sidonie Nadherny*, 181-2.
14. Rilke, letter, 1903, quoted in DE/L, 120.
15. *Lin-tsu T'an-ching*, Platform Sutra of the Sixth Patriarch, in E. Rouselle, *Sinica*, quoted in A. Watts, *The Way of Zen*, 220.
16. Gochiku, in A. Watts, 204.
17. L. Wittgenstein, *Philosophical Investigations*, 110.
18. B. Lonergan, *A Third Collection*, ed. F.E. Crowe, Paulist Press, New York, 1985, 133.
19. A. Watts, 198.
20. Arnold Bauer, 1972, 1.
21. Roman Guardini, 1961, 304.
22. Rilke, letter, May 18, 1897, in Carl Sieber, *Rene Rilke*, 1932.

BIBLIOGRAPHY

RAINER MARIA RILKE

POETRY

Sämtliche Werke, ed. E. Zinn, Insel Verlag, Frankfurt, 1955-66
Dichtung und Volkstum, ed. E. Zinn, 1939
The Book of Images, tr. E. Snow, North Point Press/ Farrar, Straus & Giroux, New York, NY, 1994
Poems From the Book of Hours, "Das Studenbuch", tr. B. Deutsch, New Directions, New York, NY, 1975
The Book of Hours, tr. Strayer, University of Salzburg Press, 1995
Rodin and Other Prose Pieces, tr. G.C. Houston, Quartet, London, 1986
Auguste Rodin, tr. Jessie Lamont & Hans Trausil, ed. Jeremy Mark Robinson, Crescent Moon, 2017
An Unofficial Rilke: Poems 1912-1926, tr. M. Hamburger, Anvil Press Poetry, London, 1981
Translations From the Poetry of Rainer Maria Rilke, tr. M.D. Herter Norton, W.W. Norton, New York, NY, 1993
New Poems, tr. J.B. Leishman, Hogarth Press, London, 1963
Rose Window and Other Verse From New Poems, Bullfinch, 1999
Poems, 1906 to 1926, tr. J.B. Leishman, Hogarth Press, London, 1957
Rilke On Love and Other Difficulties: Translations and Considerations of Rainer Maria Rilke, J.J.L. Mood, W.W. Norton, New York, NY, 1993
Requiem and Other Poems, tr. J.B. Leishman, Hogarth Press, London, 1935
Duino Elegies, tr. J.B. Leishman & S. Spender, Hogarth Press, London, 1957
Duino Elegies, tr. S. Cohn, Carcanet Press, Manchester, 1989
Duino Elegies Done Into English, Cardiff, 1941
Duino Elegies and the Sonnets To Orpheus, Boston, MA, 1977
Sonnets To Orpheus, tr. J.B. Leishman, Hogarth Press, London, 1946

RAINER MARIA RILKE

Sonnets To Orpheus, tr. L. Norris & A. Keele, Skoob Books, London, 1991
Sonnets To Orpheus, tr. R. Hunter, Hulogosi Communications, 1993
Later Poems, tr. J.B. Leishman, Hogarth Press, London, 1938
Selected Poems, tr. J.B. Leishman, Penguin, London, 1964
The Selected Poetry of Rainer Maria Rilke, tr. S. Mitchell, Picador, London, 1987
Selected Poems of Rainer Maria Rilke, tr. R. Bly, Harper & Row, New York, NY, 1981
Between Roots: Rilke, tr. R. Lesser, Princeton University Press, Princeton, NJ, 1989
Selected Works, tr. G.C. Houston & J.B. Leishman, Hogarth Press, London, 2 vols, 1954/60
The Best of Rilke, tr. W. Arndt, University Press of New England, Hanover, NH, 1989
Poems, tr. J. Lemont, Columbia University Press, New York, NY, 1943
Poems, tr. J.B. Leishman, Everyman, London, 1996
Dance the Orange: Selected Poems, tr. Michael Hanburger, ed. Jeremy Mark Robinson, Crescent Moon, 2007/ 2012
Poems, tr. Jessie Lamont, ed. Jeremy Mark Robinson, Crescent Moon, 2017
Testament, ed. E. Zinn, Frankfurt, 1975
Ahead of All Parting, Random House, New York, NY, 1997
Complete French Poems, tr. A. Paulin, Graywolf, 1987
The Notebook of Malte Laurids Brigge, tr. M.D. Herbert Norton, Norton, New York, NY, 1964
Diaries of a Young Poet, tr. E. Snow & M. Winkler, Norton, New York, NY, 1998

LETTERS

Selected Letters, 1902-1926, tr. R.C. Hull, 1946
Letters on Cézanne, ed. Clara Rilke, Cape, London, 1988
Letters To Benvenuta, tr. H. Norden, Hogarth Press, London, 1953
Letters To a Young Poet, tr. R. Snell, Sidgwick & Jackson, London, 1945
Letters To a Young Poet, tr. M.D. Herter Norton, W.W. Norton, New York, NY, 1963
Letters To Merline, 1919-1922, tr. V. & M. MacDonald, Methuen, London, 1951
Furstin Marie von Thurn und Taxis-Hohenlohe: Erinnerungen an Rainer Maria Rilke, R. Oldenbourg, Berlin, 1937
Briefewechsel Rainer Maria Rilke und Marie von Thurn und Taxis, Insel

RAINER MARIA RILKE

Verlag, Leipzig, 1951
The Letters of Rainer Maria Rilke and Princess Maria von Thurn und Taxis, tr. N. Wydenbruck, Hogarth Press, London, 1988
Briefe, 1892-1904, Insel Verlag, Leipzig, 1939
Briefe und Tagebücher aus der Frühzeit 1899-1902, Insel Verlag, Leipzig, 1931
Briefe, 1902-1906, Insel Verlag, Leipzig, 1929
Briefe, 1904-1907, Insel Verlag, Leipzig, 1939
Briefe, 1906-1907, Insel Verlag, Leipzig, 1930
Briefe, 1907-1914, Insel Verlag, Leipzig, 1933 & 1939
Briefe, 1914-1921, Insel Verlag, Leipzig, 1937
Gesammalte Briefe, 1892-1926, Insel Verlag, Leipzig, 1940
Briefe an seinen Verleger, Insel Verlag, Leipzig, 1949
Briefe aus Muzot, 1921-1926, Insel Verlag, Leipzig, 1935 & 1937
Briefe an Nanny Wunderly-Volkart, Insel Verlag, Leipzig, 1977
Briefe an eine junge Frau, Insel-Bucherei, n.d.
Briefe, vol. 1, 1897-1914, vol. 2, 1914-1926, Insel Verlag, Leipzig, 1950
Lettres à une amie venitienne, Milan, 1941
Lettres à Rodin, Paris, 1931
Rainer Maria Rilke et Merline: Correspondance, Zurich, 1954
Briefwechsel mit Benvenuta, Esslingen, 1954
Briefwechsel Rainer Maria Rilke und Lou Andreas-Salomé, Insel Verlag, 1975
Rainer Maria Rilke/ André Gide, Correspondance, 1909-1926, Paris, 1952
Correspondance Rilke/ André Gide/ Emile Verhaeren, Paris, 1955
Briefewechsel Rilke und Katharina Kippenberg, Insel Verlag, Leipzig, 1954
Briefewechsel an Sidonie Nádherny, Insel Verlag, Leipzig, 1973
Briefewechsel Rilke/ Hofmannsthal 1899-1925, Insel Verlag, Leipzig, 1978
Lettres autour d'un jardin, Paris, 1977
"Primal Sound", in H. Bloch, 1960

OTHERS

Lou Albert-Lasard. *Wege mit Rilke*, Frankfurt, 1952
Lou Andreas-Salomé. *The Freud Journal*, tr. S.A. Leavy, Hogarth Press, London, 1965
—. *Rainer Maria Rilke*, Leipzig, 1928
—. *Lebensrückblick*, ed. E. Pfeiffer, Tachenbuch 54, Frankfurt, 1974
J.-F. Angelloz. *Rilke*, Paris, 1952
Baron & Ernst, eds. *Rainer Maria Rilke: The Alchemy of Alienation*,

RAINER MARIA RILKE

University Press of Kansas, 1986

T. Bahti. *Ends of the Lyric: Direction and Consequence in Western Poetry*, John Hopkins University Press, Baltimore, MD, 1996

W.T. de Bary, et al, eds. *Sources of Chinese Tradition*, Columbia University Press, 1960

D. Basserman. *Der andere Rilke*, Bad Homburg, 1961

—. *Der späte Rilke*, Munich, 1947

A. Bauer. *Rainer Maria Rilke*, tr. U. Lamry, Ungar, New York, NY, 1972

M. Bauer. *Rainer Maria Rilke und Frankreich*, Berne, 1961

G. Bays. *The Orphic Vision: Seer Poets From Novalis To Rimbaud*, University of Nebraska Press, Lincoln, 1964

H.W. Belmore. *Rilke's Craftsmanship: An Analysis of His Poetic Style*, Blackwell, Oxford, 1954

Leo Bersani. *A Future For Astynanax*, Marion Boyars, 1978

M. Betz. *Rilke in Frankreich*, Herbert Reichner Verlag, Vienna, 1937

—. *Rilke in Paris*, Zurich, 1948

R. Binion. *Frau Lou: Nietzsche's Wayward Disciple*, Princeton University Press, Princeton, NJ, 1968

S.J. Bithell. *Modern German Literature 1880-1950*, Methuen, London, 1959

H.M. Bloch & H. Salinger, eds. *The Creative Vision: Modern European Writers*, Grove Press, New York, NY, 1960

B. Boesch, ed. *German Literature: A Critical Survey*, Methuen, London, 1971

C.M. Bowra. *Inspiration and Poetry*, Macmillan, London, 1955

B. Bradley. *Rainer Maria Rilkes Neue Gedichte. Ihr zyklisches Gefüge*, Francke Verlag, Berlin, 1967

—. *Rainer Maria Rilkes Der neuen Gedichte anderer Teil: Entwicklungsstufen seiner Pariser Lyrik*, Francke Verlag, Berlin, 1976

R. Brinkmann, ed. *Romantik in Deutschland*, Metzler, Stuttgart, 1978

Brodsky. *Russia in the Works of Rainer Maria Rilke*, Wayne State University Press, 1984

M. Brown. *The Shape of German Romanticism*, Cornell University Press, Ithaca, 1979

S. Brutzer. *Rilkes Russiche Reisen*, Stallüpönnen, 1934

E. Buddeberg. *Rainer Maria Rilke: eine innere Biographie*, Stuttgart, 1954

G. Burchheit, ed. *Rainer Maria Rilke: Stimmen der Freunde*, Freiburg, 1931

P.J. Burgard, ed. *Nietzsche and the Feminine*, University Press of Virginia, Charlottesville, 1994

S. Burnshaw *et al*. *The Poem Itself: Forty-five Modern Poets*, Schocken Books, New York, NY, 1967

E.M. Butler. *Rainer Maria Rilke*, Cambridge University Press, Cambridge, 1944

RAINER MARIA RILKE

—. *The Tyranny of Greece Over Germany*, Cambridge University Press, Cambridge, 1935
H. Cammerer. *Rainer Maria Rilke Duineser Elegien*, Stuttgart, 1937
J. Campbell. *The Power of Myth*, with B. Moyers, ed. B.S. Flowers, Doubleday, New York, NY, 1988
T. Casey. *Rainer Maria Rilke: A Centenary Essay*, Macmillan, London, 1975
E. Cassirer-Solmitz. *Rainer Maria Rilke*, Heidelberg, 1957
H. Cixous. *The Hélène Cixous Reader*, ed. Susan Sellers, Blackwell, Oxford, 1994
V.A. Conley. *Hélène Cixous*, Harvester Wheatsheaf, Hemel Hempstead, 1992
J. Cornell. *Theatre of the Mind: Selected Diaries, Letters, and Files*, ed. M.A. Caws, Thames & Hudson, London, 1993
S. Corngold. *Complex Pleasures: Forms of Feeling in German Literature*, Cambridge University Press, Cambridge, 1998
F. Dehn. *Rainer Maria Rilke und Sein Werk*, Leipzig, 1934
P. de Man. *Allegories of Reading: Figural Language in Rousseau, Nietzsche, Rilke, and Proust*, Yale University Press, New Haven, CT, 1979
—. *Blindness and Insight*, University of Minnesota Press, Minneapolis, 1983
P. Demetz. *René Rilkes Prager Jahre*, Düsseldorf, 1953
J. De Mul. *Romantic Desire in (Post)Modern Art and Philosophy*, State University of New York Press, Albany, NY, 1999
D. Dyer. *The Stories of Kleist*, Duckworth, 1977
M. Eckhart, *Selected Writings*, Penguin, London, 1994
M. Eliade. *Patterns In Comparative Religion*, Sheed & Ward, 1958
—. *Shamanism: Archaic Techniques of Ecstasy*, Princeton University Press, NJ, 1972
—. *Myths, Dreams and Mysteries*, Harper & Row, New York 1975
—. *Ordeal by Labyrinth*, University of Chicago Press, Chicago IL, 1984
—. *Symbolism, the Sacred, and the Arts*, Crossroad, New York, NY, 1985
R. Faesi. *Rainer Maria Rilke*, Zurich, 1921
J. Fletcher & A. Benjamin, ed; *Abjection, Melancholia and Love: the Work of Julia Kristeva*, Routledge, London, 1990
L. Forster, ed. *The Penguin Book of German Verse*, Penguin, London, 1958
H.-J. Frey. *Studies in Poetic Discourse: Mallarmé, Baudelaire, Rimbaud, Hölderlin*, tr. W. Whobrey, Cambridge University Press, Cambridge, 1996
S. Friedrichsmeyer. *The Androgyne in Early German Romanticism: Friedrich Schlegel, Novalis and the Metaphysics of Love*, Bern, New York, NY, 1983

RAINER MARIA RILKE

M. Froment-Meurice. *Solitudes From Rimbaud To Heidegger,* tr. P. Walsh, State University of New York Press, Albany, NY, 1995

R. Furness. *The 20th Century: 1890-1945 (The Literary History of Germany),* Croom Helm, 1978

William H. Gass. *Habitations of the Word,* Cornell University Press, Ithaca, 1997

J. Gebser. *Rilke und Spanien,* Zurich, 1945

A. Gide. *Journals 1889-1949,* ed. & tr. J. O'Brien, Penguin, London, 1967

C. Goll. *Rilke et les femmes,* Paris, 1955

W.L. Graff. *Rainer Maria Rilke: Creative Anguish of a Modern Poet,* Princeton University Press, NJ, 1956

R. Guardini. *Rilke's Duino Elegies: An Interpretation,* tr. K.G. Knight, Darwen Finlayson, 1961

W. Günther. *Weltinnenraum: Die Dichtung Rainer Maria Rilke,* Berlin, 1952

M. Hamburger. *Reason and Energy: Studies in German Literature,* Weidenfeld & Nicolson, 1970

—. *Testimonies: Selected Shorter Prose, 1950-1987,* Carcanet, 1989

—. *Collected Poems, 1941-1994,* Anvil Press Poetry, 1995

—. *The Truth of Poetry,* Anvil Press Poetry, 1996

G. Hartman. *The Unmediated Vision: An Interpretation of Wordsworth, Hopkins, Rilke and Valéry,* Yale University Press, New Haven, CT, 1954

M. von Hattingberg. *Rilke und Benvenuta,* Vienna, 1943

H. Heine. *The North Sea,* tr. E. Lazarus, Crescent Moon, 2017

E. Heller. *The Disinherited Mind,* Bowes & Bowes, 1971

J.F. Hendry. *Life of Rainer Maria Rilke: Sacred Threshold,* Carcanet, 1983

F. Hölderlin, *Poems and Fragments,* tr. M. Hamburger, Anvil Press Poetry, 1994

—. *Hölderlin's Songs of Light,* tr. M. Hamburger, ed. Jeremy Mark Robinson, Crescent Moon, 2012

H.-E. Holthusen. *Rilke,* tr. J.P. Stern, Bowes & Bowes, 1952

—. *Rainer Maria Rilke in Selbstzeugnissen und Dokumenten,* Hamburg, 1967

—. *Der späte Rilke,* Zurich, 1949

—. *Rilkes Sonnets an Orpheus,* Munich, 1937

J. Huppelsberg. *Rainer Maria Rilke: Biographie,* Munich, 1949

G.T. Hughes. *Romantic German Literature,* Edward Arnold, London, 1979

Luce Irigaray. *The Irigaray Reader,* ed. M. Whitford, Blackwell, Oxford, 1991

—. *Je, tu, nous: Toward a Culture of Difference,* tr. A. Martin, Routledge, London, 1993

K.W. Jonas. "Rainer Maria Rilkes Handschriften", *Philobiblon,* XV, 1/2,

RAINER MARIA RILKE

1971
—. "Rilke und Paul Thun-Hohenstein", *Jahrbuch des Wiener Goethe-Vereins*, 79, 1975
J. Jones. "Renewing the Dance: René Daumal, the Surrealism of the Bardo, and Shamanic Poetry", *Heaven Bone*, 11, Spring, 1994
C.G. Jung. *Memories, Dreams, Reflections*, Collins, London, 1967
R. Kassner. *Rilke: Gesammelte Erinnerungen*, ed. K. Bohenenkamp, Pfullingen, 1976
K. Kippenberg. *Rainer Maria Rilke: ein Beitrag*, Zurich, 1948
—. *Rainer Maria Rilkes Duineser Elegien und Sonnette an Orpheus*, Wiesbaden, 1946
F. Klatt. *Rainer Maria Rilke*, Vienna, 1949
D. Kleinband. *The Beginning of Terror: A Psychological Study of Rainer Maria Rilke's Life and Work*, New York University Press, New York, NY, 1995
H. Koenig. *Rilkes Mutter*, Pfullingen, 1963
S. Kofman. *The Enigma of Woman: Woman in Freud's Writings*, Cornell University Press, Ithaca, 1985
W. Kohlschmidt. *Rainer Maria Rilke*, Lübeck, 1948
K.L. Komar. *Rainer Maria Rilke: Transcending Angels*, University of Nebraska Press, 1988
D. Krell. *Lunar Voices: Of Tragedy, Poetry, Fiction, and Thought*, Chicago University Press, Chicago, IL, 1995
H. Kreutz. *Rilkes Duineser Elegien*, Munich, 1950
J. Kristeva. *The Kristeva Reader*, ed. T. Moi, Blackwell, Oxford, 1986
—. *Desire in Language: A Semiotic Approach To Literature and Art*, ed. L.S. Roudiez, tr. T. Gora *et al*, Blackwell, Oxford, 1982
—. *Tales of Love*, tr. L.S. Roudiez, Columbia University Press, New York, NY, 1987
—. *Revolution in Poetic Language*, tr. M. Walker, Columbia University Press, New York, NY, 1984
—. *Strangers To Ourselves*, tr. L.S. Roudiez, Harvester Wheatsheaf, Hemel Hempstead, 1991
W. La Barre. *The Ghost Dance*, Allen & Unwin, London, 1972
W. Leppmann. *Rilke: A Life*, tr. R.M. Stochman, Fromm International Publishing Corporation, New York, NY, 1984
A. Livingstone. *Lou Andreas-Salomé: Her Life and Works*, Moyer Bell, New York, NY, 1984
A. Mahler-Werfel. *Diaries 1898-1902*, Cornell University Press, Ithaca, NY, 1999
S. Mandel. *Rainer Maria Rilke: The Poetic Instinct*, Southern Illinois University Press, Carbondale, 1965

RAINER MARIA RILKE

E. Marks & I. de Courtivron, eds. *New French Feminisms: an Anthology*, Harvester Wheatsheaf, Hemel Hempstead, 1981
E.C. Mason. *Rilke's Apotheosis: A Survey of Representative Recent Publications on the Work and Life of Rainer Maria Rilke*, Blackwell, Oxford, 1938
—. *Rilke und Goethe*, Cologne, 1938
—. *Lebenshaltung und Symbolik bei Rainer Maria Rilke*, Weimar, 1939
—. *Rilke, Europe, and the English-Speaking World*, Cambridge University Press, Cambridge, 1961
—. *Rilke*, Oliver & Boyd, 1963
—. *Rainer Maria Rilke: sein leben und seine Werk*, Göttingen, 1964
K.M. May. *Nietzsche and Modern Literature: Themes in Yeats, Rilke, Mann and Lawrence*, Macmillan, London, 1988
D. McCort. *Going Beyond the Pairs: The Coincidence of Opposites in German Romanticism, Zen and Deconstruction*, State University of New York Press, 2001
K. Millett. *Sexual Politics*, Doubleday, Garden City, 1970
Toril Moi. *Sexual/ Textual Politics: Feminist Literary Theory*, Routledge, London, 1988
B.J. Morse. "Rainer Maria Rilke and the Occult", *Journal of Experimental Metaphysics*, 1945/6
F. Nietzsche. *Beyond Good and Evil*, Allen & Unwin, London, 1923
—. *The Will To Power*, tr. W. Kaufmann & R. Hollingdale, Vintage, 1968
—. *A Nietzsche Reader*, ed. R.J. Hollingdale, Penguin, London, 1977
Novalis. *Works* (Minor), Schlegel, Paris, 1837
—. *Hymns To the Night and Other Selected Writings*, tr. C.E. Passage, Bobbs-Merrill Company, Indianapolis, 1960
—. *Novalis Schriften. Die Werke Friedrichs von Hardenberg*, ed. R. Samuel et al, Stuttgart, 1960-88
—. *Pollen and Fragments: Selected Poetry and Prose*, tr. A. Versluis, Phanes Press, Grand Rapids, 1989
—. *Philosophical Writings*, ed. M.M. Stoljar, State University of New York Press, Albany, NY, 1997
P. Obermuller *et al*, eds. *Katalog der Rilke – Sammlung von Richard von Mises*, Frankfurt, 1966
W. O'Flaherty. *Women, Androgynes, and Other Mythical Beasts*, University of Chicago Press, Chicago, 1980
F. Olivero. *Rainer Maria Rilke: A Study in Poetry and Mysticism*, Cambridge University Press, Cambridge, 1931
C. Osann. *Rainer Maria Rilke: Der Weg eines Dichters*, Zurich, 1941
M. Payne. *Reading Theory: An Introduction To Lacan, Derrida, and Kristeva*, Blackwell, Oxford, 1993

RAINER MARIA RILKE

H.F. Peters. *Rainer Maria Rilke: Masks and the Man*, University of Washington Press, Seattle, 1960
R. Petit. *Rainer Maria Rilke in und nach Worpswede*, Worpswede, 1983
E. Pfeiffer. "Rilke und die Psychoanalyse", *Litteraturwiss, Jahrbuch der Görresgesellschaft*, 17, 1976
—. ed. *Lou Andreas-Salomé: Einstragungen, letzte Jahre*, Frankfurt, 1982
D. Prater. *A Ringing Glass: The Life of Rainer Maria Rilke*, Clarendon Press, 1994
M. Raymond. *Baudelaire au surréalisme*, Corti, 1963
P. Redgrove. *The Black Goddess and the Sixth Sense*, Bloomsbury, London, 1987
J. Reed. *Bitter Blue: Tranquillisers, Drugs, Dependency*, Peter Owen, 1995
—. *Angels, Divas & Blacklisted Heroes*, 1999
Rilke en Valais, Suisse Romande, 3, 4, 1939
Rilke et la France, Hommages et souvenirs, Paris, 1943
A. Rimbaud. *Complete Works, Selected Letters*, tr. W. Fowlie, University of Chicago Press, Chicago, 1966
W. Ritzer. *Rainer Maria Rilke*, Vienna, 1951
J. Rolleston. *Rilke in Transition*, Yale University Press, New Haven, CT, 1970
—. *Narratives of Ecstasy*, Wayne State University Press, 1987
W. Rose & G. Craig Houston. *Rainer Maria Rilke: Aspects of His Mind and Poetry*, 1938
H. Rosenberg, *The Tradition of the New*, Da Capo Press, New York, NY, 1994
E. Sagarra & P. Skrine, eds. *A Companion To German Literature*, Blackwell, Oxford, 1997
L.S. Salzberger. *Hölderlin*, Cambridge University Press, Cambridge, 1952
N. Saul. *History and Poetry in Novalis and in the Tradition of the German Enlightenment*, Institute of Germanic Studies, 1984
I. Schnack. *Rilkes Leben im Werk und Bild*, Insel Verlag, Wiesbaden, 1957
—. ed. *Rainer Maria Rilke: Chronik seines Lebens und seines Werkes*, Frankfurt, 1975
E. Sewell. *The Structure of Poetry*, Routledge & Kegan Paul, London, 1951
—. *The Orphic Voice: Poetry and Natural History*, Routledge, London, 1961
E. Showalter, ed. *The New Feminist Criticism*, Virago, London, 1986
R. Schröder. *Rainer Maria Rilke*, Zurich, 1952
C. Sieber. *René Rilke: Die Jugend Rainer Maria Rilke*, Leipzig, 1932
A. Silvaire. *Rainer Maria Rilke: Inédits, études et notes*, Paris, 1952
E. Simmenauer. *Rainer Maria Rilke: Legende und Mythos*, Berne, 1953
E.L. Stahl. *Rainer Maria Rilke: Aspects of His Mind and Poetry*, Sidgwick & Jackson, London, 1938

RAINER MARIA RILKE

E. Starkie. *Arthur Rimbaud*, Faber, London, 1973
J. Steiner. *Rilkes Duineser Elegien*, Munich, 1969
A. Stephens. *Rainer Maria Rilke's Gedichte an die Nacht: an essay in interpretation*, Cambridge University Press, Cambridge, 1972
J.P. Stern: *The Heart of Europe: Essays on Literature and Ideology*, Blackwell 1922
J.W. Storck. *Rainer Maria Rilke als Brieschreiber*, Freiburg, 1957
L. Stryk, ed. *The Penguin Book of Zen Poetry*, Penguin, 1981
S.R. Suleiman. *Subversive Intent: Gender, Politics and the Avant-Garde*, Harvard University Press, Cambridge, MA, 1990
—. *Risking Who One Is*, MIT Press, Cambridge, MA, 1995
Tao Te Ching, tr. D.C. Lau, Penguin, London, 1963
R. Taylor. *The Romantic Tradition In Germany*, Methuen, 1970
M. Travers. *An Introduction To Modern European Literature*, Macmillan, London, 1998
F.M. von Thurn und Taxis-Hohenlohe. *Erinnerungen an Rainer Maria Rilke*, Insel-Bücherei, Frankfurt, 1966
P. Valéry. *An Anthology*, ed. James Lawler, Routledge, London, 1977
F.W. van Heerikhuizen. *Rainer Maria Rilke: His Life and Work*, 1951
P. Verlaine. *Œuvres poétiques complètes*, ed. Y.-G. Le Dantec, Gallimard, 1951
A. Watts. *The Way of Zen*, Penguin, London, 1962
D. Weisshart, ed. *Translating Poetry: The Double Labyrinth*, Macmillan, London, 1989
F. Werfel. "Begegnungen mit Rilke", *Sudentenland*, 18, 1976
Ludwig Wittgenstein: *Tactatus Logico-Philosophicus*, Routledge 1961
—. *Philosophical Investigations*, tr. G.E.M. Anscombe, Blackwell 1968
M.R. Witzling. *Voicing Our Visions: Writing by Women Artists*, Women's Press, London, 1992
H. Wocke. *Rilke und Italien*, Giesen, 1940
H. Wohltmann. *Rainer Maria Rilke in Worpswede*, Hamburg, 1952
E.V. Wolfenstein. *Inside/Outside Nietzsche*, Cornell University Press, 2000
F. Wood. *Rainer Maria Rilke: The Ring of Forms*, University of Minnesota Press, Minneapolis, 1958
Richard Woods, ed. *Understanding Mysticism*, Athlone Press, London, 1980
N. Wydenbruck. *Rilke: Man and Poet: A Biographic Study*, John Lehmann, 1949
P. Zech. *Rainer Maria Rilke*, Dresden, 1930
M. Zermatten. *Les Dernières annés de Rainer Maria Rilke*, Fribourg, 1975
—. *Der Ruf der Stile: Rilkes Walliser Jahre*, Zurich, 1954
—. *Les Années valaisannes de Rilke*, Sierre, 1951

RAINER MARIA RILKE

E. Zinn. *Dichtung und Volkstum*, 40, 1939
S. Zweig. *Abscheid von Rilke*, Tübingen, 1927

In the Dim Void

Samuel Beckett's Late Trilogy: *Company, Ill Seen, Ill Said* and *Worstward Ho*

by Gregory Johns

This book discusses the luminous beauty and dense, rigorous poetry of Samuel Beckett's late works, *Company, Ill Seen, Ill Said* and *Worstward Ho*. Gregory Johns looks back over Beckett's long writing career, charting the development from the *Molloy-Malone Dies-Unnamable* trilogy through the 'fizzles' of the 1960s to the elegiac lyricism of the *Company* series. Johns compares the trilogy with late plays such as *Ghosts, Footfalls* and *Rockaby*.

Bibliography, notes. Illustrated. 120pp
ISBN 9781861712974 Pbk and ISBN 9781861712608 Hbk
9781861713407 E-book

Beauties, Beasts, and Enchantment

CLASSIC FRENCH FAIRY TALES

Translated and with an Introduction by Jack Zipes

A collection of 36 classic French fairy tales translated by renowned writer Jack Zipes. *Cinderella*, *Beauty and the Beast*, *Sleeping Beauty* and *Little Red Riding Hood* are among the classic fairy tales in this amazing book.
Includes illustrations from fairy tale collections.
Jack Zipes has written and published widely on fairy tales.

'Terrific... a succulent array of 17th and 18th century 'salon' fairy tales'
- *The New York Times Book Review*

'These tales are adventurous, thrilling in a way fairy tales are meant to be... The translation from the French is modern, happily free of archaic and hyperbolic language... a fine and sophisticated collection' - *New York Tribune*

'Enjoyable to read... a unique collection of French regional folklore' - *Library Journal*

'Charming stories accompanied by attractive pen-and-ink drawings' - *Chattanooga Times*

Introduction and illustrations   612pp.   ISBN 9781861712510 Pbk   ISBN 9781861713193 Hbk

MAURICE SENDAK
& the art of children's book illustration

Maurice Sendak is the widely acclaimed American children's book author and illustrator. This critical study focuses on his famous trilogy, *Where the Wild Things Are*, *In the Night Kitchen* and *Outside Over There*, as well as the early works and Sendak's superb depictions of the Grimm Brothers' fairy tales in *The Juniper Tree*. L.M. Poole begins with a chapter on children's book illustration, in particular the treatment of fairy tales. Sendak's work is situated within the history of children's book illustration, and he is compared with many contemporary authors.

Fully illustrated. The book has been revised and updated for this edition.
ISBN 9781861714282 Pbk   ISBN 9781861713469 Hbk

CRESCENT MOON PUBLISHING

web: www.crmoon.com e-mail: cresmopub@yahoo.co.uk

ARTS, PAINTING, SCULPTURE

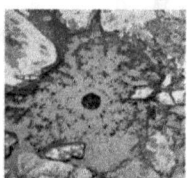

The Art of Andy Goldsworthy
Andy Goldsworthy: Touching Nature
Andy Goldsworthy in Close-Up
Andy Goldsworthy: Pocket Guide
Andy Goldsworthy In America
Land Art: A Complete Guide
The Art of Richard Long
Richard Long: Pocket Guide
Land Art In the UK
Land Art in Close-Up
Land Art In the U.S.A.
Land Art: Pocket Guide
Installation Art in Close-Up
Minimal Art and Artists In the 1960s and After
Colourfield Painting
Land Art DVD, TV documentary
Andy Goldsworthy DVD, TV documentary

The Erotic Object: Sexuality in Sculpture From Prehistory to the Present Day
Sex in Art: Pornography and Pleasure in Painting and Sculpture
Postwar Art
Sacred Gardens: The Garden in Myth, Religion and Art
Glorification: Religious Abstraction in Renaissance and 20th Century Art
Early Netherlandish Painting
Leonardo da Vinci
Piero della Francesca
Giovanni Bellini

Fra Angelico: Art and Religion in the Renaissance
Mark Rothko: The Art of Transcendence
Frank Stella: American Abstract Artist
Jasper Johns
Brice Marden

Alison Wilding: The Embrace of Sculpture
Vincent van Gogh: Visionary Landscapes
Eric Gill: Nuptials of God
Constantin Brancusi: Sculpting the Essence of Things
Max Beckmann
Caravaggio
Gustave Moreau

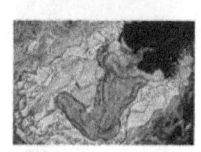 

Egon Schiele: Sex and Death In Purple Stockings
Delizioso Fotografico Fervore: Works In Process 1
Sacro Cuore: Works In Process 2
The Light Eternal: J.M.W. Turner
The Madonna Glorified: Karen Arthurs

LITERATURE

J.R.R. Tolkien: The Books, The Films, The Whole Cultural Phenomenon
J.R.R. Tolkien: Pocket Guide
Tolkien's Heroic Quest
The *Earthsea* Books of Ursula Le Guin
Beauties, Beasts and Enchantment: Classic French Fairy Tales
German Popular Stories by the Brothers Grimm
Philip Pullman and *His Dark Materials*
Sexing Hardy: Thomas Hardy and Feminism
Thomas Hardy's *Tess of the d'Urbervilles*
Thomas Hardy's *Jude the Obscure*
Thomas Hardy: The Tragic Novels
Love and Tragedy: Thomas Hardy
The Poetry of Landscape in Hardy
Wessex Revisited: Thomas Hardy and John Cowper Powys
Wolfgang Iser: Essays and Interviews
Petrarch, Dante and the Troubadours
Maurice Sendak and the Art of Children's Book Illustration
Andrea Dworkin
Cixous, Irigaray, Kristeva: The *Jouissance* of French Feminism
Julia Kristeva: Art, Love, Melancholy, Philosophy, Semiotics and Psychoanalysis
Hélène Cixous I Love You: The *Jouissance* of Writing
Luce Irigaray: Lips, Kissing, and the Politics of Sexual Difference
Peter Redgrove: Here Comes the Flood
Peter Redgrove: Sex-Magic-Poetry-Cornwall
Lawrence Durrell: Between Love and Death, East and West
Love, Culture & Poetry: Lawrence Durrell
Cavafy: Anatomy of a Soul
German Romantic Poetry: Goethe, Novalis, Heine, Hölderlin
Feminism and Shakespeare
Shakespeare: Love, Poetry & Magic
The Passion of D.H. Lawrence
D.H. Lawrence: Symbolic Landscapes
D.H. Lawrence: Infinite Sensual Violence
Rimbaud: Arthur Rimbaud and the Magic of Poetry
The Ecstasies of John Cowper Powys
Sensualism and Mythology: The Wessex Novels of John Cowper Powys
Amorous Life: John Cowper Powys and the Manifestation of Affectivity (H.W. Fawkner)
Postmodern Powys: New Essays on John Cowper Powys (Joe Boulter)
Rethinking Powys: Critical Essays on John Cowper Powys
Paul Bowles & Bernardo Bertolucci
Rainer Maria Rilke
Joseph Conrad: *Heart of Darkness*
In the Dim Void: Samuel Beckett
Samuel Beckett Goes into the Silence
André Gide: Fiction and Fervour
Jackie Collins and the Blockbuster Novel
Blinded By Her Light: The Love-Poetry of Robert Graves
The Passion of Colours: Travels In Mediterranean Lands
Poetic Forms

POETRY

Ursula Le Guin: Walking In Cornwall
Peter Redgrove: Here Comes The Flood
Peter Redgrove: Sex-Magic-Poetry-Cornwall
Dante: Selections From the Vita Nuova
Petrarch, Dante and the Troubadours
William Shakespeare: Sonnets
William Shakespeare: Complete Poems
Blinded By Her Light: The Love-Poetry of Robert Graves
Emily Dickinson: Selected Poems
Emily Brontë: Poems
Thomas Hardy: Selected Poems
Percy Bysshe Shelley: Poems
John Keats: Selected Poems
John Keats: Poems of 1820
D.H. Lawrence: Selected Poems
Edmund Spenser: Poems
Edmund Spenser: Amoretti
John Donne: Poems
Henry Vaughan: Poems
Sir Thomas Wyatt: Poems
Robert Herrick: Selected Poems
Rilke: Space, Essence and Angels in the Poetry of Rainer Maria Rilke
Rainer Maria Rilke: Selected Poems
Friedrich Hölderlin: Selected Poems
Arseny Tarkovsky: Selected Poems
Arthur Rimbaud: Selected Poems
Arthur Rimbaud: A Season in Hell
Arthur Rimbaud and the Magic of Poetry
Novalis: Hymns To the Night
German Romantic Poetry
Paul Verlaine: Selected Poems
Elizaethan Sonnet Cycles
D.J. Enright: By-Blows
Jeremy Reed: Brigitte's Blue Heart
Jeremy Reed: Claudia Schiffer's Red Shoes
Gorgeous Little Orpheus
Radiance: New Poems
Crescent Moon Book of Nature Poetry
Crescent Moon Book of Love Poetry
Crescent Moon Book of Mystical Poetry
Crescent Moon Book of Elizabethan Love Poetry
Crescent Moon Book of Metaphysical Poetry
Crescent Moon Book of Romantic Poetry
Pagan America: New American Poetry

MEDIA, CINEMA, FEMINISM and CULTURAL STUDIES

J.R.R. Tolkien: The Books, The Films, The Whole Cultural Phenomenon
J.R.R. Tolkien: Pocket Guide
The *Lord of the Rings* Movies: Pocket Guide
The Cinema of Hayao Miyazaki
Hayao Miyazaki: *Princess Mononoke*: Pocket Movie Guide
Hayao Miyazaki: *Spirited Away*: Pocket Movie Guide
Tim Burton : Hallowe'en For Hollywood
Ken Russell
Ken Russell: *Tommy*: Pocket Movie Guide
The Ghost Dance: The Origins of Religion
The Peyote Cult

Cixous, Irigaray, Kristeva: The *Jouissance* of French Feminism
Julia Kristeva: Art, Love, Melancholy, Philosophy, Semiotics and Psychoanalysis
Luce Irigaray: Lips, Kissing, and the Politics of Sexual Difference
Hélène Cixous I Love You: The *Jouissance* of Writing
Andrea Dworkin
'Cosmo Woman': The World of Women's Magazines
Women in Pop Music
HomeGround: The Kate Bush Anthology
Discovering the Goddess (Geoffrey Ashe)
The Poetry of Cinema
The Sacred Cinema of Andrei Tarkovsky
Andrei Tarkovsky: Pocket Guide
Andrei Tarkovsky: *Mirror*: Pocket Movie Guide
Andrei Tarkovsky: *The Sacrifice*: Pocket Movie Guide
Walerian Borowczyk: Cinema of Erotic Dreams
Jean-Luc Godard: The Passion of Cinema
Jean-Luc Godard: *Hail Mary*: Pocket Movie Guide
Jean-Luc Godard: *Contempt*: Pocket Movie Guide
Jean-Luc Godard: *Pierrot le Fou*: Pocket Movie Guide
John Hughes and Eighties Cinema
Ferris Bueller's Day Off: Pocket Movie Guide
Jean-Luc Godard: Pocket Guide
The Cinema of Richard Linklater
Liv Tyler: Star In Ascendance
Blade Runner and the Films of Philip K. Dick
Paul Bowles and Bernardo Bertolucci
Media Hell: Radio, TV and the Press
An Open Letter to the BBC
Detonation Britain: Nuclear War in the UK
Feminism and Shakespeare
Wild Zones: Pornography, Art and Feminism
Sex in Art: Pornography and Pleasure in Painting and Sculpture
Sexing Hardy: Thomas Hardy and Feminism

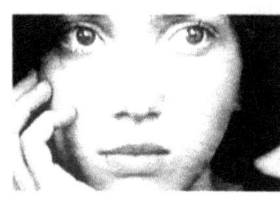

The Light Eternal is a model monograph, an exemplary job. The subject matter of the book is beautifully organised and dead on beam. (Lawrence Durrell)
It is amazing for me to see my work treated with such passion and respect. (Andrea Dworkin)

CRESCENT MOON PUBLISHING
P.O. Box 1312, Maidstone, Kent, ME14 5XU, Great Britain. www.crmoon.com

cresmopub@yahoo.co.uk   www.crescentmoon.org.uk

www.ingramcontent.com/pod-product-compliance
Lightning Source LLC
Chambersburg PA
CBHW070158100426
42743CB00013B/2956